CW00493926

1

ISBN: 9798444152249

Cover design by Ben Doughty

Edited by Natalie Bleau

Printed in United Kingdom

THE FIFTH KING

The Rise and Fall of Wilfred Benitez

Ben Doughty

"Don't let this bum lick you..!" implored the old guru with sombre disgust. Context notwithstanding, it was a 'reach.' Much of what is uttered in the corner would not be admissible in a court of law but - even by the standards of motivational chutzpah - Ray Arcel had to know that his implication was slanderous at best. In any event, despite the trainer's good intentions, history will show that Roberto Duran was not inspired to any noticeably greater effort as he dropped a unanimous decision to the handsome, honey skinned prodigy who might have thwarted the aim of a heat seeking missile in his best incarnation. 23 years old and only once mastered by the incomparable Sugar Ray Leonard, Wilfred Benitez could not have known that his crowning glory would also be the 'Last Hurrah.' 40 years on, the WBC junior middleweight title fight in Las Vegas is seen not so much as the high point of the victor's career but as a temporary slump in the storied affairs of the loser.

As the ringside hacks began to pen their obituaries for the greatest lightweight of the colour TV era, only a man denuded of his faculties by the ingestion of hallucinogenic drugs would have predicted that 'Manos De Piedra' would enjoy a more illustrious trajectory thereafter. Having vanquished arguably the greatest constituent of boxing's fabled 'Mount Rushmore', Benitez would never claim another notable scalp. Rather, he would become one.

Throw a stick at boxing and you will hit 6 tragedies by accident. Take Richard Green, the referee that night, as a case in point. 18 months later he would take his own life - some say on account of the residual guilt emanating from his professional involvement in the ill fated Ray Mancini - Deuk - Koo Kim fight from which the latter never regained consciousness. For Wilfred Benitez there would come a point at which even suicide was not an option since the ravages of the only profession he had ever known had robbed him of the physical wherewithal to carry out the fatal deed unassisted. Acknowledging his impotence in that regard it is said that he once asked his sister and carer, Yvonne, to put an end to his purgatorial misery with a gun. Whether the story is true or was merely concocted by a journalist seeking to wring extra pathos from an entry level of sadness, it seems unlikely that the situation has radically improved since the allegation appeared in print.

Wilfred Benitez is not the only fighter to pay a terrible price for innumerable years of shipping expertly flung leather but the obscurity to which he has been confined seems especially undeserved. While his more feted contemporaries - Duran, Leonard, Hearns and Hagler - have suffered mixed fortunes in retirement, collectively, they have been immortalised as 'The Four Kings'; regal monarchs of perhaps the deepest era in boxing history. Rightly or wrongly, that sacred cow status has never been extended to a man who fought 3 of the Kings and defeated one at a relative canter. It is not my contention that he is quite on par with the legendary quartet since ultimate greatness in the squared circle seems to demand a 'Second Act' - or the robust longevity of a Joe Louis - but if Marvin, Tommy, Ray and Roberto were the main event then 'El Radar' was definitely the chief support. Unfortunately, in addition the dramatic fall from grace, exists the probability that his brilliance was a tad harder to appreciate - in the same way that John Coltrane is harder to appreciate than 'The Beatles.' With no snobbishness intended, it has taken this connoisseur more than a half a lifetime of immersion in the 'sweet science' to fully comprehend how frighteningly good Benitez was at an age when most of us are contemplating our first driving lesson. That such a creature was not possessed of the emotional maturity to balance his physical genius is hardly astonishing when all said and done. And so alongside the glittering triumphs came dips in form, automobile crashes and the seemingly mandatory misappropriation of funds that ought to have been saved for a rainy day. A spent force at the ripe old age of 25, he would still be exploited half a dozen years later - following an extended period of inactivity that included a bizarre 14-month hiatus in Argentina that remains shrouded in mystery.

For a sport that demands so much from its protagonists, boxing hardly excels in the realm of aftercare. If great tennis players, for instance, wound up in such routinely awful circumstances then it would surely lead to ripples of concern. And whilst not every professional fighter ends his days in a fog of cerebrally diminished penury, the examples are too numerous for the collective boxing fraternity to be entirely absolved of guilt. Nonetheless, this book does not seek to draw attention to the plight of a 'forgotten man.' One couldn't plausibly claim that Wilfred Benitez has been forgotten since, at the very least, he will always be the answer to a popular trivia question. As the youngest world champion in the annals of pugilism his niche in posterity is unlikely to be usurped but the permanence of that legacy provides scant mitigation for the plain fact that his story has never been told.

1/ IN THE NAME OF THE FATHER

Since the earliest days of my involvement in boxing, almost numberless are the fighters who have uttered that well worn phrase when expounding upon the importance of their fistic mentor. "He's like a father to me," goes the familiar refrain. Often a coach assumes the role as a much needed surrogate in the life of a wayward street kid, bound for the worst case scenarios of the ghetto until salvation comes in the shape of tough love and arduous routine. Sometimes the axis may sour due to any number of factors but the innately honourable nature of the quasi - paternal bond is seldom called into question. Strange then perhaps that whenever a fighter of note is trained by his actual father, the relationship is tinged with dysfunction as often as not.

The pushy, unfulfilled parent who seeks to live vicariously through an offspring is a common theme in boxing and beyond. Perhaps he felt destined for ring glory himself until injury or circumstances intervened or perhaps he couldn't fight a lick and so determines that his son(s) must atone for nature's tragic omissions. On occasion, the father was a credible contender who didn't quite reach the mountain top and 'junior' inherits the obligation either willingly or otherwise. Such alliances have varied from highly successful to poignantly catastrophic, but few have escaped the collateral damage that comes with obsession.

In the case of Gregorio Benitez Sr. fate initially seemed hell bent on nipping his dreams in the bud - quite literally - by blessing him with 4 consecutive daughters.

Persevering in the time honoured fashion of poor immigrant families, Gregorio and Clara continued to let nature take its course until she had borne him 4 boys, thus providing the raw material for his proxy ambitions. Gregorio Jr, Frankie, Alphonso and Wilfred would all don gloves before shedding their milk teeth and perhaps Evelyn, Kleo, Yvonne and Mary can be thankful for the abject lack of trajectory that female boxing had in the 1960s. 50 years later, the patriarch of the family might have been tempted to hedge his bets.

Gregorio 'Goyo' Benitez was born on May 24, 1928 in Puerto Rico. Although there is no documented evidence of him ever boxing competitively, by his own account, Papa Benitez participated in more than 300 unsanctioned bouts on the street during his teenage years for which he received the subsidies of nickels and dimes from the impromptu spectators who would gather ad hoc. Exaggeration or not, it was a format he wouldn't forget when the time came to season his own brood in the basic tenets of gloved combat almost 2 decades later. In 1948, aged 19, Gregorio moved to New York City, finding employment at an auto body shop in the South Bronx where he worked as a repairman and paint specialist. Seemingly by design, Goyo had escaped his homeland shortly before the enactment of 'Law 53' - better known as the 'gag law' - which made it illegal to own or display a Puerto Rican flag or to express public support for the growing Independence Movement. The subsequent scenes of revolt saw over 3,000 people arrested and a blizzard of deaths as the Island became a hotbed of unrest and political violence. The discord would last for 9 years until Law 53 was repealed in 1957 on the basis that it was unconstitutional. [1]

During an interview with Boxing News in 1981, Gregorio claims to have married Clara Elena Rosa in 1947 although it's conceivable that his recollection was a tad premature. Regardless, having 'tied the knot,' the two wasted no time in starting a family. The girls arrived with roughly annual frequency until first born son, Gregorio Jr, entered the world in February, 1955, followed by Alphonso in May, 1956, and Frankie on July 14, 1957. Wilfred, the youngest of the Benitez clan, was born on September 12, 1958 and was permitted an 'incubation' period of 5 years before he was obliged to swap punches with any semblance of venom. Perhaps not fully absorbed by the business of spray-painting cars and fixing hubcaps, Goyo began to frequent the New York gyms and became a regular at fight cards staged at Madison Square Garden or the Sunnyside Garden Arena in Queens. Sometimes he would earn a few extra dollars as an assistant second and when boxing insiders sought to question his pedigree in later years, he would cite the diligence of his study in the golden era:

"I went to the big fights and saw how others fight. I learned to hit the belly from Marcel Cerdan. The 'Bolo Punch' from Kid Gavilan. I watch Sugar Ray Robinson and learn the hook from him - right to the body, double up on the hook."

By 1963 he was staging neighbourhood 'smokers' in the schoolyard attached to PS 124 in the Bronx near East Tremont Avenue and East 177th Street. It is said that he would delineate the 'ring' with a piece of chalk before drumming up trade in the manner of a carnival barker,

---

[1] Source: 'Malfunctioning Radar" – Jose Corpas, April 2017

charging 50c cents to a dollar for 'admission' depending on market forces on any given afternoon. Having attracted up to a hundred paying punters on a good day, Goyo would challenge other local youths to glove up and take on any one of his 4 sons, including 5-year-old Wilfred who was often required to slug it out with boys 2 or 3 years his senior. Sometimes Wilfred fought twice for the reward of a dollar, his designated share of a 'gate' that might have come to 75 bucks. Perhaps it was an early introduction to the fight game's creative economics.

The backstreet brawls continued until the summer of 1966, when Goyo took the decision to move the family back to Puerto Rico - citing the overabundance of crime and bad influences in New York as the reason for the exodus. "Too much dope, too much trouble. I told them we go home where it is not so bad," he explained retrospectively, despite cynical claims that the move had more to do with perpetuating the abuse to which his sons were subjected, unlicensed scraps and all. Empowered by his sense of mission, Goyo built a gym at the back of the single storey yellow stone house in St Just, a small barrio in the Trujillo Alto district some 20 odd miles south of San Juan. Thereafter, he imposed a relentless regime from which none of the boys were exempt. Gregorio, the eldest at 11 years old, was instructed to pound the rustic roads at 4am every morning and it wasn't long before 8-year-old Wilfred began to tag along. "He would stop halfway through the running and tell me that he was going back," remembered Gregorio. "I would tell him, 'It's too dark for you to go home alone. You came out with me and you have to go back with me.'" The story goes that Gregorio became something of a secondary mentor to his youngest brother as the two sparred innumerable rounds in the smaller than regulation sized ring, acquiring the subtle nuances of the 'Noble Art' by trial and error. "Wilfred used to cry to my father that he couldn't catch me or hit me." said Gregorio. "I told him, 'Do the same things I do.' Everything you told him to do, he did it."

According to legend, Wilfred had his first amateur fight that same year, aged 7 and a half and scaling 62 pounds wringing wet. The identity of his opponent in what is described as the Puerto Rican Golden Gloves is unknown but the result is said to have been a draw. Draws in amateur boxing are uncommon and often feature in the fanciful stories of the taproom charlatans who wax lyrical about their erstwhile fistic prowess but - by the spring of 1967 - Wilfred was regularly competing in junior tournaments and soon became accustomed to the ritual of having his hand raised in victory. Nevertheless, at this early stage, he was not considered to be the most talented or likely to succeed of the brothers. Said mantle was carried by Gregorio, who had reportedly racked up a record of 51-6 by 1968 before going on to win a National Junior Golden Gloves title at bantamweight in 1969.

In 1970, the family moved to a new house and the back garden gym set up was immediately replicated. A journalist from Sports Illustrated who paid a visit in 1976 - not long after Wilfred became the youngest champ in history - described it as having 'the look of a small airplane hangar' with 'yellowing newspaper clippings, old fight photographs and posters on the clean white walls.' In the further interests of creating a mental picture, our scribe itemised 2 rubdown tables, 3 punch bags and a homemade ring juxtaposed with the chickens who ran freely in the small yard that separated the makeshift training area from the family home. At this point, Goyo's quest for a champion had extended beyond the fruit of his own loins as future stars, Alfredo Escalara, Esteban DeJesus and Carlos De Leon gravitated to his tutelage by word of mouth. Research encourages one to believe that sparring sessions between DeJesus and the 12-year-old Wilfred were especially full blooded - despite a 9 year age gap - and even the cruiserweight De Leon wasn't deemed out of bounds, since Goyo believed that a fighter must harden himself against bigger adversaries in rehearsal for battle. Finding his feet in such a rugged eco system might well have informed the youngest son's fabled defensive genius but there is also little doubt that the brain and body of a child were exposed to a surfeit of adult punishment on a regular basis.

In early February of 1970, Gregorio was considered favourite to win the featherweight division in the Puerto Rican Golden Gloves, having boosted his log to 122-14 by the time of the tournament's commencement. Much to his father's enduring chagrin however, he was bested in the quarter finals by one Luis Rodriguez thus forfeiting a berth on the national team and an opportunity to compete in the Central American and Caribbean Games in Panama City at the end of the month. Disgusted with his 15-year-old son's sub-par performance, Goyo opted to turn him professional without delay but not before making his feelings on the matter abundantly clear:

"You embarrassed me in front of all my friends. I will never forgive you."

2/ 'CANNON FODDER AND MANGO PICKERS'

On Sunday April 5, 1970, 2 months after his 15th birthday, Gregorio Benitez Jr. made his professional debut in San Juan. His opponent, one Rivera Cintron, had lost his only previous recorded contest and presented no major problems as Gregorio cruised to 4 round points win. By the time of his first 10 rounder on April 3, 1972, one source credits the eldest Benitez boy with a record of 19-0, compiled against 'a litany of cannon fodder and mango pickers' but the admittedly fallible boxrec database only lists 5 sanctioned fights for him in that same 2-year period. Statistical anomalies aside, Gregorio came through his first test, decisioning the oft beaten Angel Rivera at the Hiram Bithorn Stadium on a show that was headlined by former World Heavyweight Title challenger, Joe Roman, who was cast against Jose Manuel Urtain, the reigning European champ. Although clearly too good for second and third raters, Gregorio suffered from a bow-legged condition that sometimes caused his feet to become entangled when moving from side to side. To counteract this natural handicap, Goyo simply advised his son to stand and trade with opponents as opposed to boxing at a distance and relying on movement. Allied to that default strategy, a lack of concussive power meant that the undefeated junior lightweight prospect was taking more punches than might have been considered ideal, even when facing 'also rans.' Irrespective of Goyo's projections, it seemed unlikely that he was destined for longevity in the ring.

Off the back of the Rivera win, Gregorio landed an opportunity to showcase his skills in the world boxing capital of New York, in a scheduled 6 rounder at the Felt

Forum, the 5000-seater arena underneath Madison Square Garden. With the entire Benitez contingent in attendance, he earned a hard fought unanimous decision over an Ecuadorean trial horse who went by the name of Taco Guilleromo, much to the delight of his partisan kinfolk. Apparently not so easily impressed, the old man was seen to strike his son at the bout's conclusion before launching into a stream of invective regarding the precise nature of Gregorio's shortcomings - as evidenced by his inability to deal more decisively with a man who took his name from a folded tortilla. In hindsight, perhaps Goyo ought to have been more upbeat about what turned out to be his eldest son's last win, in New York or anywhere else. The unbeaten record was snapped 6 and a half weeks later when Eduardo Santiago nicked a majority decision at Gregorio's expense over 4 rounds at the Singer Bowl in Flushing. Being narrowly pipped by Santiago - a former National A.A.U and NY Golden Gloves champ- was no shame in itself but more worrying was the ease with which he had 'caught' punches, as if the mere concept of defence represented a conniving effeminacy.

Goyo surmised that more training was the answer and put Gregorio through an intensive 4-month camp with exclusively bigger sparring partners and drills to improve his balance. Also in camp was world ranked lightweight, Esteban DeJesus, as he readied for his chance to crash the big time in a non-title 10 rounder vs reigning WBA champion, Roberto Duran. The fight was set for Friday, November 17 at Madison Square Garden and with Gregorio looking to return to winning ways on the undercard it amounted to the biggest night of Goyo's boxing life at that time. Duran, an emergent superstar of the sport, was undefeated in 31 starts but DeJesus caused a sensation when he decked the Panamanian in the opening round and outboxed him thereafter to pull off Ring Magazine's 'Upset of The Year.' If the occasion had represented Esteban's 'coming out party' then it was also Gregorio's swansong as he came off second best to the highly useful Dominican, Vilomar Fernandez, in a 6 round prelim about an hour before the main event.

A ringside source on the night claimed that Fernandez was just too 'cute' for Gregorio, catching him with 'right hand sucker punches' from the first bell. A right hand/ left hook combination sent him to the mat in Round 4 and - rising on unsteady legs - he fell to the deck once more without being hit, shortly before the bell. He tasted the canvas again in the fifth, courtesy of a lead right, but managed to survive the round by virtue of moving and clinching before taking a steady pummelling in the last stanza. There was no doubting the lopsided verdict in Villomar's favour and - at the ludicrously tender age of 17 and a half - Gregorio's career was over. Shirking any admission of accountability, Goyo blamed the sorry saga on Mother Nature and the diminishing effects of love and romance.

"They can say what they want but I retired Gregorio because he was bow legged. He'd try to move quickly and he'd fall down. Then he got married and wanted to fight some more. But I say 'No.' I told him marriage makes you too weak. You are retired."

Hereafter, Gregorio would help Goyo train his brothers and the large stable of fighters his father had accumulated by the tail end of 1972. Whatever he may have gained in the way of remuneration or self esteem during his brief stint as a professional fighter, it seems unlikely that the pros outweighed the cons. Some say he was 'a walking mess' at 28 and by the early 90s it was confirmed that the oldest of the brothers was suffering from brain damage - alternatively known as dementia pugilistica or chronic traumatic encephalopathy. Given the brevity of his stats on boxrec, one has to assume that much of the damage came from punches for which he received little or no recompense, from the schoolyard in the Bronx, to the Benitez back garden and his hundred plus amateur fights in Puerto Rico. If a legendary old stager like Archie Moore should have found himself a tad forgetful in the twilight years, it would not have caused astonishment but Gregorio Benitez Jr didn't deserve such a fate. And his misfortune was portentous of things to come.

By the time Gregorio bowed out, Wilfred was 14 and fast cutting a swathe as a fully fledged amateur boxing prodigy. In January 1972, in a tournament held on the Caribbean Island of Sint Maarten, he represented Puerto Rico at Flyweight and sensationally beat the highly touted Cuban, Douglas Rodriguez, an imminent bronze medallist at the Munich Summer Olympics. If he genuinely came into existence on September 12, 1958 then Wilfred would have been 13 years old at the time of this implausible triumph over a world class fighter whose 21st birthday was already several months behind him. Even allowing for the legitimate concept of early physical maturity, such a chasm in age engenders a healthy scepticism in the neutral observer. Could Wilfred Benitez have been older than history has claimed as part and parcel of his singular achievements...?

Recalling the time he paired the supposedly 16-year-old Wilfred with Al Hughes at the Felt Forum in September,

1974, the storied MSG matchmaker, Teddy Brenner, explained: "He had a baptismal birth certificate that said he was older. I didn't know how young he really was." To place the situation in context, Goyo would have needed to convince Brenner and the NYSAC that his youngest son was at least 18 in order to box professionally in New York - and the same applied to Gregorio Jr and Frankie who also fought in the hallowed building underaged. Other points of reference that seek to put years on our hero include a USA vs Puerto Rico international team match at the Paterson Armory just before Christmas, 1972 during which he was described as '16 year old bantamweight sensation, Wilfredo Benitez.' 7 months later, on July 21st 1973, he beat Canada's Camille Huard in the North American Boxing Championships in Milwaukee, an event that was screened on Network TV in the States. In the crackling footage that appears on YouTube, the ABC commentator is heard to say, "In the white shirt from Puerto Rico, 17 years of age, Wilfredo Benitez... He's a student from the town of Carolina..." In deference to the birth date that his family have always celebrated, Wilfred(o) looks absurdly youthful on screen, although the levels of boxing savvy and physical strength he exhibits en route to outpointing his capable 19-year-old opponent in a torrid battle merely add to the confusion.

The extra vowel attached to his Christian name was not entirely incidental. The presumably fake baptismal birth certificate - which claimed he was 16 in 1972 - was issued in the name of Wilfredo and contributed to a fudge that prevailed for many years after the subject became an established star. Further exacerbating the uncertainty, Goyo would often refer to his son as Wilfredo because it was 'easier to pronounce' and records at the old school in the Bronx list a Wilfredo Benitez who was born in 1956 amongst its former alumni. Perhaps it was always Goyo's plan to fast track his last born to the upper echelons of the fight game and the lucrative rewards that came with the territory. All things considered, it seems most likely that the young starlet's age was falsified in order to facilitate his entry into senior competition and the ruse was maintained until it was no longer important and, indeed, detracted from his remarkable feats.

After shocking Rodriquez at the beginning of the year, Wilfred won the Puerto Rican Bantamweight title by virtue of beating Roberto Roman Guzman in July, 1972. Still not 14, he was too young for Olympic competition - even by the testimony of the bogus baptismal certificate - but continued to take on world class seniors in peripheral tournaments. In November, 1972 he lost a 4-1 decision in the 119 lb semi-final of the Central American and Caribbean Championships to eventual winner, Orlando Martinez, the reigning Olympic Champion who had beaten future world champ, Alfonso Zamora, to earn the distinction. Although not victorious, it was another yardstick for his insanely precocious development, both technically and physically. The only notable stoppage loss Wilfred appears to have suffered in compiling a claimed amateur record of 123-6 came in January 1973 at the hands of subsequent super bantamweight contender, Derrick Holmes, in a tournament that pitted the USA vs The Caribbean. Holmes, a vaunted banger from Washington DC, would go on to stop another embryonic Puerto Rican great when he iced Wilfredo Gomez inside a round the following year- although he was unable to replicate that feat in a 1980 WBC title challenge, by which time Gomez had blossomed into the most formidable 122 pounder the world has ever seen.

Following the loss to Holmes, Wilfred stepped up to featherweight and split 2 fights with former victim Roberto Guzman before scoring an upset points win over world ranked Canadian, Dave Anderson, in May 1973. With his sights set once more on the Central American and Caribbean Championships scheduled for November, the 'wunderkind' straddled another division, eventually losing in the Puerto Rican lightweight final to Jose Luis Vellon in October. It is said that Benitez and Vellon defeated each other 2 times apiece but, on this occasion, the reversal cost Wilfred the opportunity to represent his island in Ciudad, Mexico in a competition that also featured a teenaged Mike McCallum and the great Cuban Heavyweight, Teofilo Stevenson. The fact that Vellon went on to win the tournament might well have rubbed salt in the wounds of deflation but there was little time for introspection as Goyo plotted the next move. Concluding that the boy had served his apprenticeship - and was perhaps a little 'long in the tooth' for recreational boxing - it was decreed that he would turn pro, 10 weeks after his 15th birthday. For whatever the opinion of a manipulated man - child might be worth, Wilfred endorsed the decision a number of years later in an interview with William Nack for Sports Illustrated:

"In the amateurs, I was 15 years old and fighting older men. And I was boxing and beating them all. Why shouldn't I become a professional..?"

3/ TANK TOWN

Wilfred took his first paid bow on November 22, 1973 at a nameless venue in San Juan. His opponent, Hiram Santiago, might have excelled at any number of vocations but the stock in trade of a prize-fighter was apparently not amongst them as he folded in the opening round. There are no fight reports depicting the exact nature of the stoppage and Boxrec lists no previous or subsequent experience for Santiago beyond the less than 3 minutes he shared with a burgeoning legend. Reportedly, the winner received $100. Also on the card was Wilfred's immediately older brother, Frankie, who outpointed Tony Tris over 6 to score his 10th win in a row whilst Esteban DeJesus dispatched Seattle club fighter, Al Foster, inside a round in the top liner. Perhaps the biggest puncher of the Benítez boxing dynasty, the 16-year-old Frankie had been obliged to go the distance for the second time running since turning over 7 months earlier.

8 days later Wilfred stopped debutant Jesse Torres in two rounds on Sint Maarten before the brothers appeared once again on a DeJesus undercard in the first week of January 1974. On a Monday night at the newly constructed Coliseo Roberto Clemente, Frankie and Wilfred swept aside unremarkable opposition in two and four rounds respectively before the star of Goyo's 'portfolio' stopped former WBA light welterweight king, Alfonso 'Peppermint' Frazer with a sweet left hook in the final frame of a 10 rounder. Adding a liberal pinch of spice to the proceedings was the fact that Frazer hailed from Panama and was managed by Carlos Eleta who also handled the affairs of the nation's favourite fighting son.

Forswearing revenge on behalf of Panama in general and Roberto Duran in particular, Eleta concluded: "DeJesus is good but not good enough to take my other fighter. They are scheduled to meet in Panama on the 16th of March and Duran will KO him."

Wilfred crammed in two more early wins against debutants before Frankie - who was rumoured to enjoy the pleasures of the flesh a tad more than an aspirational fighter should - received his comeuppance on April Fool's Day at the hands of Laudiel Negron, a hard hitting light welterweight who had represented Puerto Rico at the 1972 Olympics. A mere lightweight himself, Frankie started fast in an effort to get rid of his man but had evidently punched himself out by the fourth round. Running on empty, he was floored by a big right hand in the sixth, after which Negron unloaded a relentless barrage that compelled Goyo to throw in the towel. Given compelling evidence that he was not the most protective of fathers, one can only assume that his offspring was in receipt of a frightful battering to demand such drastic action. Lest the disappointment of his first pro loss should prove insufficient, Papa Benitez allegedly withheld Frankie's $400 purse by way of censuring his lack of due diligence in preparation. "Frankie didn't train properly for this fight so he doesn't deserve to get any money," he decreed.

On the same card, Wilfred went the distance for the first time without a vest - outpointing Victor Mangual over 8 rounds - and hopefully got to keep his wages. Aside from being the first man to extend Wilfred Benitez to the final bell, the only outstanding thing about Mangual was the bizarre symmetry of his record, having had 3 previous bouts against the same opponent - resulting in a win, a loss and a draw. In U.S fight circles they call it the 'Tank Town' circuit and there are suggestions that Wilfred had several fights in his first year of punching for pay that are not listed on Boxrec - including 'smokers' in the Netherlands Antilles were regulation was lax at best. At the time of his first appearance in New York in September 1974 - vs trial horse Al Hughes at the Felt Forum - his official record stood at 11-0 with 10 KOs but some sources claim another 20 odd unsanctioned affairs had fallen under the radar.

Already known to Puerto Rican fight fans in the Big Apple, Wilfred stopped Hughes in the fifth of an 8 round main event on a Monday evening that fell 4 days after his 16th birthday. Curiously, having had two rehabilitative wins since the Negron debacle, Frankie outpointed Hughes' twin brother, Bobby Joe, on the same night as previewed in the New York Times on September 15, 1974:

'Two brothers will fight two brothers at the Felt Forum tomorrow night when Frankie Benitez of Puerto Rico, a lightweight, meets Bobby Hughes and Wilfredo Benitez, a welterweight, meets Al Hughes. The Hughes brothers are twins. The Benitez brothers have similar won/lost records - Frankie is 12-1 with 10 knockouts and Wilfredo's is 11-0 all by knockout. Preliminary fights begin at 8 o' clock.'

Implausible as it may seem, the theme continued a month later at Madison Square Garden proper when Wilfred halted tough Canadian, Terry Summerhays, in six rounds and Frankie took care of Summerhays' brother, Johnny, in an identical time frame. According to reports, Terry provided a stern test for the younger Benitez prior to getting nailed in the conclusive session with a devastating right hand that sent him careering into the ropes where he was bombarded without mercy until the ref waved it off. The exultant Puerto Rican punters in the house had yet more reason to be cheerful when Frankie produced one of his best performances, boxing beautifully for five rounds before dishing out a severe drubbing to his outgunned adversary in the 6th. With Johnny unable to answer the bell for Round 7, it was left to Gary Summerhays to complete a hat trick of misfortune for the family as he wound up on the short end of a majority decision in an over the weight light heavyweight battle with Pedro Soto. On the subject of weight, Wilfred scaled 144 pounds on the day of his fight and was clearly a light welter, despite the description in the NY Times that placed him a division above.

The boys were back at the Felt Forum in early December, as Wilfred took on another Canadian in Lawrence Hafey, a veteran of 52 fights with a respectable tally of 39 wins. The film shows Wilfred (announced as Wilfredo) clad in royal blue trunks accompanied in ring centre by camp aide, Jaran Manzaret, who sports a white second's jacket and a buoyant Afro. In the first round he moves with a nonchalant liquid grace, seemingly disinterested in the stocky pressure fighter who bears a passing resemblance to the ill fated Billy Collins Jr but struggles to launch a meaningful offensive. During the interval, Don Dunphy - the Dean of boxing broadcasters in the golden age - informs ABC viewers that 'Wilfredo' was born on October 5 1955, thus making him 19 by process of logical deduction. The smokescreen of his age notwithstanding, Wilfred 'wakes up' in Round 2 and proceeds to put on a spellbinding display of pugilistic poetry, comprising a rapier left jab and fluid combinations - fired from both stances with the imperious poise of a mountain gazelle. Not limited to the attributes of a 'Fancy Dan', the 'man boy' also exhibits a spiteful body attack and power in either hand that might have accounted for a less seasoned foe, particularly in the last round when Benitez suddenly seems intent on closing the show. Showing faith in his durability if nothing else, it appears that Hafey eventually stops even trying to avoid the triple left hooks that come his way before the bell calls time on his stoic masochism. Tony Castellano had it a clean sweep at 8 rounds to nothing whilst referee, Arthur Mercante, and judge, Bernie Friedkin, somehow managed to find two rounds in favour of the man from Nova Scotia - likely on the premise of his wholly ineffective aggression.

Conducting the post-fight interview through an interpreter, Wilfred extended his gratitude to the Puerto Rican fans, "... that are here in New York and even the ones that didn't come to the fight." With Gregorio retired, the burden of Goyo's vision now rested squarely on his shoulders - and those of Frankie, who went over old ground on the show, decisioning Bobby Joe Hughes again in another 8 rounder. Alphonso, the second oldest son, seems to have slipped through the net of his father's obsession after some initial conflict regarding his career ambitions. Although he showed promise and reportedly reached the quarterfinals of the 1972 Puerto Rican Golden Gloves, Alphonso didn't much care for boxing or the rigours of training and informed his father that he wished to go to college to become an electrical engineer. Some say Goyo expelled him from the family home in disgust before coming around to the idea on the proviso that he partake in an unsanctioned bout on the island of St. Croix in order to raise funds for the books he required for his academic studies. According to the story, Alphonso was victorious and picked up a $200 purse by way of reward.

"He knocked the guy out in the fourth round," claimed Goyo. "I gave him the money. I say, 'Here, go buy your books. You have just retired.'"

4/ FRANKIE GOES TO PALOOKAVILLE

Wilfred commenced 1975 with three stoppages over opponents with losing records before being taken 10 rounds for the first time in his career by undefeated rookie, Santos Solis. Hailing from a well known boxing family that included the world class trio of Julian, Enrique and Rafael, Santos appears to have given Wilfred more trouble than expected and was even adjudged the winner on one of the judge's cards. On the same Monday night in San Juan, Frankie scored a 10 round points win over the useful Black American, Brooks Byrd, who had previously KOd Laudiel Negron in 7 rounds. Although he had not entirely adopted the habits of a Trappist monk and was rumoured to be indulging in narcotics, Frankie appeared to be back on track after the Negron hiccup as he ascended the lightweight rankings.

The busy schedule continued on June 9 when Wilfred met the vastly experienced Cuban road warrior, Angel Robinson Garcia at Ramon Loubriel Stadium. In a paid career stretching back to 1955, Garcia had racked up almost 230 fights and shared a ring with such luminaries as Esteban DeJesus, Roberto Duran, Ken Buchanan and Jose Napoles along the way. Despite being matched historically tough across the length and breadth of the world, he had a 60 percent winning record and was no respecter of hype or reputations. The significance of his 10-round points loss to the Wonder Kid from Carolina would take a while to marinate but it was another notch on the bedpost of arguably the finest elite level journeyman in boxing history. Wilfred or Wilfredo, depending on the documentation, was officially 19- 0 and streaking towards a world title shot at the earliest opportunity.

That total had swelled to 23-0 by the time the Benitez brothers returned to the Felt Forum on October 20 and experienced diametrically opposing fortunes. Wilfred disposed of an Argentine southpaw called Omar Reuben Realecio in 6 rounds while Frankie lost a 10-round decision to the lightly regarded Chris Fernandez, who had been brought in as a 'safe' opponent for the now world ranked Puerto Rican, thought to be on the cusp of a title shot. With both Duran and WBC title holder, 'Guts' Ishimatsu, in his sights, the Benitez brain trust were not inclined to take any chances. Unfortunately, Fernandez - who happened to be a southpaw - hadn't read the script and largely frustrated his bigger punching, more aggressive opponent to win 8 out of 10 rounds on the card of referee, George Coyle. In the aftermath, Goyo had no trouble in identifying the problem:

"Frankie just doesn't want to train. He stays out late at night and chases too many girls. It finally caught up with him tonight. He thinks he can just go out there and knock everybody out with one punch. He should have beaten this guy easily."

As if to demonstrate where Frankie had gone wrong, Wilfred avenged the loss on his behalf at the Roberto Clemente Coliseum on December 13 in what amounted to an unofficial eliminator for Antonio Cervantes' WBA light welterweight crown. That Fernandez had somehow earned a Top 10 ranking at 140 off the back of beating his brother seemed a tad generous but the sanctioning bodies have never been renowned for their integrity and logic when all is said and done. In truth, the New York based Dominican was a club fighter who had lost 3 on the spin - including a 4th round KO defeat at the hands of

Rocky Mattioli - before derailing Frankie against the run of play. Be it down to the vagaries of genetics or a lack of debilitating vices, Wilfred was a better fighter than his elder sibling circa 1975 and duly sailed to another 10-round points victory before a crowd of 9000. With the New Year beckoning, he was 25-0 with 20 KOs and on the verge of realising his father's dream - provided that Cervantes could be persuaded to put his laurels on the line against the teenage sensation next time out.

As Wilfred moved closer to the pinnacle of ultimate glory, Frankie drifted in the opposite direction; losing for the second time in succession on the undercard. On this occasion, he was outpointed by Josue Marquez - a useful Puerto Rican light welter who had taken Cervantes to a split decision in a world title challenge 2 and a half years earlier. Reports say it was a close, hard fought affair with Marquez's greater work rate and relative freshness 'down the stretch' providing the margin of victory. As the decision was announced, it was left to ringsider, Roberto Duran, to summarise to cost of this latest setback, a week before he put his title on the line against Leoncio Ortiz at the same venue:

"I wish Frankie had won because I wanted a chance to knock him out in Puerto Rico in front of his family and friends. "

With his chances of a championship fight receding, Frankie clawed back a degree of pride in holding Marquez to a draw in April, 1976 but any positive spin that might have been attached to the result was invisible to Goyo who lamented, "The kid doesn't like to train and he hates the gym. He had this bout won and he let Josue steal it from him." Having failed to register a win in his last 3 starts, Frankie 'The Terror' rebounded with a split decision over Mustapha Ali (who also went by the alias of 'TNT Gordon') in Sint Maarten before allegedly being arrested on the island for a drug related offence after the fight. It is said that Goyo used whatever leverage he had with the local authorities to ensure that his son was released without further legal ramifications but the outlook was bleak from there on in. Fighting another 4 times between 1976 and 1980, Frankie was beaten thrice and knocked out twice before fading into obscurity and dissolution.

Relocating back to the South Bronx for a spell he appears to have been consumed by the street life of using and dealing whilst generally garnering the reputation of a 'loose cannon.' On more than one occasion he was busted for possession only to receive a lenient 'slap on the wrist' perhaps in part due to his former notoriety and connections to the influential 'bigwigs' at Madison Square Garden. After getting arrested whilst already on probation, it is thought that Frankie served a brief stint in the slammer after which he drifted in and out of contact with the family before disappearing altogether for 8 years between 1984 and 1992. Thereafter, he moved back to his mother and father's house in Carolina, by all accounts depleted from years of drug addiction and the cerebral damage incurred as a result of the blows he received in the ring.
For the benefit of those who might struggle with elementary mathematics; he was 35 years old.

5/ HIGH SCHOOL REUNION

The naysayers - and those who purported to hold a card in the compassionate guild - were predictably appalled. Goyo had ruined Gregorio and Frankie and now he would serve up his youngest son as a sacrificial lamb to an all-time great who had already spurned the presumptuous advances of 10 would be claimants to his share of the World Light Welterweight Championship. Admittedly, it wasn't hard to empathise with such reservations. Although his luminous talent was obvious to a blind man on a runaway horse, there was nothing on paper to suggest that Wilfred was remotely prepared to unseat a champion of Cervantes' calibre when the fight was announced for the Hiram Bithorn Stadium in the Puerto Rican capital on March 6. The most credible names on his record belonged to Garcia and Hafey whilst Cervantes - a grown man of 30 - had fought and beaten a 'who's who' of the division, including DeJesus, 'Peppermint' Frazer and the legendary Argentinian, Nicolino Locche. If Wilfred's formative years had been tough then Antonio's rearing on the streets of Cartagena, where he shined shoes and sold contraband cigarettes in order to avoid starvation, had been demonstrably tougher.

"I lived in Chambacu, a poor neighbourhood," he recounted. "They called it 'El Corral De Negros' (The Black Yard.) It was a rough neighbourhood but a hard working town. We all had to work. It not we do not eat. I did what I needed to do, along with my family, to survive. Shining shoes was my source of income. Back then, everyone had to take care of their shoes and I would be there to give you the best shine around. The cigarettes were more underground and I would make up as much money as possible there, selling to anyone and everyone."

He was introduced to boxing by an uncle who also bestowed upon him his enduring nickname; 'Kid Pambele.' After only 3 amateur bouts, Cervantes made his professional debut in 1964, 2 years before a 7-year-old Wilfred contested his first amateur fight. Thereafter, his road to the top was fraught with obstacles as 'The Kid' suffered several defeats - including 4 in a row between September'66 and April '67 - that might have discouraged a less resilient human being. When the big opportunity came in his 41st outing, it ended in disappointment as the almost supernaturally evasive Locche retained his WBA title over 15 rounds in Buenos Aires. After Locche lost his crown to Alfonso Frazer the following year, Cervantes journeyed to Panama City and kayoed the new champion in the tenth round by way of usurpation. Subsequently, 10 successful defences had established him as the greatest Colombian fighter in history and an idol to his countrymen. A 4-1 favourite over Benitez, he was no stranger to fighting in his opponent's back yard - having recently plied his trade in Japan, Argentina, Panama, Puerto Rico and his adopted home of Venezuela.

Despite the general air of pessimism, not everybody in the business subscribed to the notion that Goyo was the worst matchmaker since Lord Raglan ordered the Charge of the Light Brigade. "His father is one of the best trainers around. He's a Vince Lombardi," opined Teddy Brenner with reference to the legendary Green Bay Packers coach who had passed away a few years earlier. Regardless of whether one endorsed such a lofty assessment, there seemed little doubt that the term 'Svengali' might have been coined for Papa Benitez and his abject intolerance of

33

dissent among the ranks. "If the father had told Wilfred to jump off a burning building, he'd have jumped," said Brenner.

Whilst his preparation presumably fell shy of such suicidal obedience, Wilfred trained relentlessly for 2 months ahead of his bid to become the youngest world champion in boxing history. Goyo would later admit it was 'the best he ever trained' before a dwindling work ethic came to characterise his pre-fight habits. Apparently focussed on glory for its own sake, Wilfred pledged to give the $7500 purse - totalling chump change even by mid 70s norms - to his father as a token of appreciation. "He told me, 'I don't want the money. I want to be champion. Make me a champion..!'" the latter explained. Undeterred by the existing champion's vastly greater experience or the gulf in age, Wilfred shrugged, "I've been fighting bigger and older guys since I was 8. So what's new..?" In camp, he sparred numerous rounds with Frankie, who at 5 foot 6 was hardly a doppelgänger for the gangling Cervantes but Goyo had a ready response for the unbelievers who sought to question his expertise:

"Some people learn by competing. I learn by observing. In New York, I went to all the big fights and I see how others work, how others fight. I studied every trainer, every big fighter. For 5 years I worked in the amateurs before my first son turned professional. I've worked over 3000 fights, amateur and professional."

On the night, as the principals awaited their introduction to a boisterous crowd of around 20 thousand, another of Goyo's former pupils could be seen cutting shapes on the sky-blue canvas with the carefree ebullience of a reigning world champ on a welcome night off. Sporting a natty double denim ensemble and the seemingly mandatory Latin Afro of the day, WBC Junior Lightweight Champion, Alfredo 'El Salsero' Escalara, shuffled and twirled to the beat of the cheery salsa music that blared through the tannoy as if to justify his nom du guerre. As he approached Cervantes' corner in the standard protocol of bonhomie, the champion sat calmly on his stool a la Joe Louis - before Sugar Ray Robinson popularised the more animated prefight jig. Benitez, looking equally relaxed in white trunks with a cyan blue trim, raised his arms aloft in acknowledgment of the roar that greeted his name. His smooth torso resembled that of a lightweight compared with his opponent's darker and more muscled skinny frame but the cocksure adolescent mojo made up for any aesthetic difference as they came together in ring centre. Goyo massaged his son's shoulders during the referee's instructions whilst Kid Pambele hunched and looked downwards, as if to conceal his true height.

Although both are listed as 5 foot 10 by historical sources, Cervantes appeared several inches taller when the bell rang - in part due to Wilfred's habit of sitting on his back foot and inviting the other man's lead, like a kid teasing a Rottweiler on a chain. The class gap that many had alluded to was nowhere to be seen in the first round as Benitez boxed with an unruffled aplomb that suggested he didn't know the difference between the WBA Champion and some of his less illustrious victims. A hundred seconds in, Cervantes tries a left hook to the body before Wilfred misses with a counter hook but compensates by spinning the champion 180 degrees with his left forearm. It was a manoeuvre worthy of an 80-fight veteran but perhaps Antonio put it down to beginner's luck as he continued to stalk his prey impassively. At the bell, Wilfred dropped his hands and stood motionless for a split second before strolling back to the corner with the studied languor of a secondary school delinquent rolling up for detention. With several of his former high school classmates in attendance, his comportment seemed oddly appropriate.

The crowd became excitable midway through the second round when Benitez scored with a leaping straight left, followed by a double jab/ straight right before circling away as Cervantes followed him around the ring, upright and methodical. The champion looked strangely lethargic and although not all of Wilfred's attacks were finding the target, even punches that landed on Cervantes' gloves were heralded like the decisive goal in a World Cup final. Antonio started the third with a greater sense of urgency, landing a hard right hand but missing with the intended follow up of a mid-range uppercut and a slashing left hook. Unperturbed, Benitez continued to score with that piston like jab, waving his gloves on occasion to mask his offensive intentions. Suddenly switching to a southpaw stance, he landed a beautiful 3 punch combination - head/ body/ head - serving a reminder that his genius was ambidextrous. In truth, there wasn't much between them but 'El Radar' - the name ascribed to the hypnotic upper body movement that made him almost diaphanous in the ring - was building a narrative of victory with the aid of a partisan crowd.

Rounds 4 through 7 followed an essentially similar pattern with Benitez landing the more eye catching flurries while Cervantes remained in lukewarm pursuit. As fine a fighter as he was, Kid Pambele was plainly not comfortable with an opponent who didn't come to him and was able to nullify his jab. Perhaps he set some store by that hoary old maxim that the challenger must 'take the title' but by the end of the 8th, the Colombian was being soundly outboxed and had failed to win a single round beyond argument. Sporting a large glob of vaseline underneath his right eye, Cervantes targeted Wilfred's body in the ninth but came off worst on the inside as the fans hailed the latter's every success with a deafening clamour. Appearing almost resigned to the status of ex - champion, Antonio hacked away in the tenth and eleventh rounds but was continually befuddled by the spellbinding craft of a young maverick who was now oozing more confidence than a Republican candidate in Wyoming. When Benitez turned his man on the ropes shorty before the bell, the two traded wildly in what amounted to the best single exchange of the fight.

Cervantes might have won the twelfth as Wilfred coasted and took a breather and the champion produced his best work in Round 13, his aggression and persistence finally paying dividends albeit rather late in the day. Benitez regained control in the fourteenth, having gotten his second wind, before clocking out with a combination of showboating, punching and defensive wizardry in the last round. At this point 'experience' was simply a euphemism for old age as the gulf in speed and freshness had become a veritable chasm. When the bell sounded, the combatants embraced momentarily before Wilfred was hoisted aloft by Goyo and several of his aides as armed police and assorted gate crashers engulfed the ring. The salsa music recommenced and the more emboldened members of the audience jostled for position whilst awaiting official confirmation of a verdict that could only go one way by any fair minded arbitration.

The first card was announced in the challenger's favour by a margin of 147-142 but Jesus Celis - not incidentally a

Venezuelan- had somehow managed to plump for Cervantes with a score of 147 - 145. The expectant throng booed before the casting vote of referee, Isaac Herrera, was made public:

"EL JUEZ Y REFEREE, HERRERA, VOTA CIENTO CUARENTA Y QUATRO - CIENTO CUARENTA Y OCHO... SENORAS Y SENORES... DE PUERTO RICO EL NUEVO CAMPEON: WILFREDO BENITEZ..!"

During the wild celebration that ensued, someone amongst a teeming mass of well wishers placed a flimsy but glittering silver crown on the new champion's head. In the mid-1970s, nobody made a big deal of brandishing the sanctioning body baubles and so what looked like a cast off from a grade school nativity play became the immediate symbol of his implausible triumph. Ultimately, it made perfect sense:

Despite the sparsity of his summers, 'El Radar' had taken Kid Pambele to school.

6/ A FORK IN THE ROAD

2 weeks after his historical victory, the champion was back in Goyo's 'National Gym' readying for another Colombian adversary in the shape of Emiliano Villa, a lanky southpaw from Barranquilla. Like Wilfred, Villa had been a highly touted amateur, reportedly racking up 124 wins against 9 losses in addition to representing Colombia in the 1972 Olympics where he lost a split decision in the second round to Britain's Graham Moughton. Unlike Wilfred, he knew the taste of defeat as a professional. An 8th round TKO at the hands of Alfonso Frazer in his 12th paid outing had been one of three reversals and second to last time out he had lost a reportedly 'razor thin' decision to Nicolino Locche at Luna Park. The World Boxing Association, who ranked Villa fourth in the pecking order of light welterweight contenders, was evidently not inclined to penalise him too heavily for what might have been a hometown 'squeeze' and duly endorsed Benitez' first title defence on May 31, 1976.

On Friday May 28, award winning journalist, Pat Putnam, described Wilfred's final sparring session - 3 days before his second 15 rounder in 8 weeks. By the writer's account, he undergoes 10 rounds with 4 different spar mates, including a 180-pound fighter by the name of Francisco Alvarez - with every round approximating a 'war.' Even by the filter of the non pampered old school, such strenuous activity 72 hours before a world title fight raised eyebrows but odder still was the fact that none of said sparring partners were southpaws like Wilfred's opponent. With no time for such 'kindergarten' logic, Goyo was quick to allay any implicit doubts about his competence.

"Right or left, Villa is made to order for the champion. It will be a tough fight for Villa has a strong chin but he comes in straight and catches almost everything. Besides, the champion can fight as a southpaw if he wants."

At the weigh in - on the day of the fight in accordance with pre 90s protocol - Villa's manager, Tabacito Sanz, expressed his reservations about fighting a Puerto Rican in Puerto Rico. 'Did the WBA have the power to reverse a hometown decision..?' he asked Bill Brennan, the governing body's official in charge. "Don't worry about it," Goyo is said to have snapped. "This isn't Panama or Argentina. They don't give us nothing here."
And then cryptically, "If there's a hometown decision, you'll get it."

Several hours later, in the familiar surroundings of the Roberto Clemente Coliseum, Benítez entered the ring sporting bright red trunks with red and white striped socks worn high over red suede boots. His chosen attire excepted, one was inclined to presume he wouldn't be in the red in any immediate financial sense due to the $60,000 purse he would receive for his first appearance as champion. Villa, wearing traditional white shorts with black trim, enjoyed his best round in the opening 3 minutes according to Putnam before finding himself on the wrong end of a 'shutout.' From the second round onwards, Benítez dominated with his immaculate left jab and constantly punished the challenger with straight rights to head and body - the textbook favoured offensive against a left-handed fighter. By the seventh round 'only great courage kept Villa up' wrote Putnam and it was that same inborn quality that spurred him to go for broke in the final round, knowing that a KO was his only chance of victory. Not inclined to play it safe and sit on an unassailable lead, Wilfred engaged his opponent toe to toe for the last 120 seconds as the two swapped hammering blows with no thought for defence.

Predictably, the score lines were wider than the Grand Canyon, with Rudy Ortega and Wally Schmidt marking 149 - 137 and 148 - 137 respectively. Referee, Ismael Falu, saw it 150 to 138 which meant that Villa had failed to win a round in the third man's estimation. "Can anyone doubt he is a champion now..?" asked Goyo rhetorically. "And now we have to plan ahead. Duran..? Yes, we want Duran. He has been having too much trouble making the lighter weight but he will have to pay to fight us. And Kid Pambele wants another fight. It will cost him some money, too."

4 and a half months elapsed before Wilfred stepped back into the ring, his longest spell of idleness since putting on the gloves as an infant. Some say this was the turning point at which Goyo lost control of his prodigy - when his word ceased to be inviolate. Taking inflation into account, perhaps the 60 grand he pocketed for the Villa fight - even allowing for substantial deductions - engendered a sense of solvency and independence that was previously unknown. In the weeks preceding his second defence, against Brockton fringe contender Tony Petronelli, rumours abounded that Wilfred - a growing boy of 18 - was struggling to make 140 and had been knocked out in sparring by a 2-fight novice called Domingo Ayala. His No. 2 ranking with the WBA notwithstanding, Petronelli was what the American scribes called a glorified club fighter but perhaps he would find himself in the right place at the right time. Trained by his father and uncle, the latterly famous Petronelli brothers who would steer

Marvin Hagler to immortality, Tony boasted a record of 35-1-1 but hadn't beaten anybody to justify his lofty position. A year earlier he had been slated to challenge Angel Espada for the WBA Welterweight strap before a broken hand forced his withdrawal.

As it happened, any suspicions that Petronelli would spring an upset looked absurdly optimistic as the New Englander was battered to a standstill inside 3 rounds on a rainy Saturday night in San Juan. The first 6 minutes were sprightly and competitive until Benitez hurt his man with a right hand / left uppercut at the end of the second and followed up with a fusillade of punches at the bell. 25 seconds into the third frame, Petronelli was felled by a huge left hook and ought to have taken a moment to recover his senses. Opting instead to jump up at the count of 2, the challenger was driven to a neutral corner and pummelled with a two-fisted malevolence until the referee's intervention at 0.53 of the round. Significantly, at the outset of the contest, commentator Don Majeski had described Wilfred as 'only 18 years of age' and also 'the youngest world champion in history.' Although people still called him Wilfredo, the October '55 birthdate had evidently been discarded now that the ruse was no longer necessary.

"Nobody expected you to beat Cervantes and, certainly, nobody expected you to win so easily tonight. What did you think about Petronelli..?" asked Majeski in the post-fight interview..?" Responding with an improved command of English, Wilfred surmised, "This fight was supposed to go 8 rounds but when I hit that guy, Petronelli, I thought 'Oh man, he's mine...!'.... And I think Pambele is gonna' do down, too."

A Cervantes rematch was scheduled for December 4 but when Wilfred almost drove his most recently acquired trophy car off the edge of a cliff in the Cordillera Central Mountain range, the WBA initially agreed to a 30 day postponement. Crashing into a pair of providentially situated trees, Wilfred suffered lacerations to his hands and bodily bruising sufficient to demand a period of recuperation. Whilst the trees had saved his life, they couldn't save his laurels when, in January 1977, the WBA took the decision to strip him of the title - ostensibly for refusing to face Cervantes as mandated. Some thought Goyo had no intention of granting Kid Pambele another crack at his son and political sympathy clearly lay with the Colombian who recaptured the vacant crown on June 25, 1977 thus further cementing his status as an all-time great. Still recognised as the 'lineal World Light Welterweight Champion' in the State of New York, Benitez was finding it increasingly difficult to sweat his burgeoning frame down to 10 stone and resolved to test the waters 7 pounds north.

The perfect record incurred its first blemish on February 2, 1977 and - with all due respect to a good fighter in Harold Weston Jr. - Wilfred only had himself to blame. After 7 closely contested rounds in which he generally had the edge, Benitez began to clown and showboat - much to the displeasure of a previously well disposed 11, 000 crowd at Madison Square Garden. Talking to his opponent ('It almost looks as if he's singing' observed MSG announcer John Condon) windmilling his right hand and presenting a Latin interpretation of the Ali shuffle suddenly took precedence over punching in the last 3 rounds. And when Wilfred did resolve to let his hands go, he punctuated the combinations with theatrical noises of percussion whilst Weston continued his dogged efforts unperturbed. 'Baby Harold' might have stolen the 10th round but still looked fortunate to wind up with a majority draw thanks to Harold Lederman and Al Reid who each had the contest all square at 5-5. Referee Johnny Lo Bianca saw it for Benitez by a margin of 7-3 which seemed closer to reality but as the patrons booed vociferously it was difficult to ascertain which fighter's grievance they sought up to uphold.

Weston thought he had done enough to win but remained under no illusion regarding the quality of the man with whom he had shared the spoils:

"He's about the trickiest and best defensive fighter I ever fought. You can throw 25 or 30 punches and you might not even hit with one. I was shocked. He planted himself on the ropes and I never expected any man in the world could get away from me on the ropes."

Perhaps the first tell-tale signpost in a career that serves as a prototype for skulduggery, came when Don King presented the bold new concept of the United States Boxing Championships. In tune with the surge of American patriotism after the Montreal Olympics, the shock haired one partnered with Ring Magazine and ABC to bring a nationally televised tournament intended to crown an undisputed U.S champ in each division. Seeking to build the perfect narrative for the American Dream, King opted to stage the third quarter-final before a captive audience at the Marion Correctional Institute in Ohio on March 6, 1977. In the late 60s he had famously served a 4-year sentence for manslaughter at M.C.I and was returning a decade later as living proof that even the most stigmatised criminal could make good in the free world - provided he found the appropriate environment for his larcenous tendencies.

With the aftertaste of the Weston blip still lingering, Wilfred entered the tourney at 147 amidst a line-up that also included Randy Shields and Floyd Mayweather Sr. His opponent, a tough Texan trial horse by the name of Melvin Dennis, provided admirable resistance but a points loss to an all-time great for the delectation of Joe Louis and around 1300 inmates was the only story his grandchildren were ever likely to hear. Benitez cruised to an 8 round decision that should have seen him advance to the semi - finals before King's tournament imploded the following month in a hail of well founded accusations of record falsifying, bogus rankings, fight fixing and payola. Various heads rolled in the resultant fallout, including that of New York State Athletic Commission

Chairman James Farley Jr, but King's distinctive noggin was not among them as he simply passed the buck to his associates. It was a well worn modus operandi that would earn him the nickname 'Teflon Don' in due course, such was his apparent inability to reap bad karma.

After a brace of first round wins - over official debutant Roberto Gonzalez and former two-time victim, Easy Boy Lake - Wilfred defended the last remnant of his world title at 140 vs Ray Chavez Guerrero at Madison Square Garden on August 3, 1977. Guerrero, a Venezuelan based in Quebec, resembled a 1950s throwback but fought like a millennial UK journeyman behind a slippery 'Philly Shell' defence that kept him in the ring if not in the fight. Benitez, who had predicted another first round knockout, finally caught up with his man in the 15th and final session of a rather desultory contest which drew constant boos from an underwhelmed crowd. Putting the punters and the challenger out of their collective misery, an innocuous left jab seemed to hurt Guerrero who staggered backwards into a neutral corner where Benitez proceeded to rain 25 unanswered blows on a defenceless, exhausted foe who eventually sprawled face first onto the bottom rope. Arising at the count of 7 but plainly in no fit state to continue, 'Jose Ray' was spared from further punishment by referee, Arthur Mercante, with 79 seconds remaining. In the eyes of the NYSAC and anyone who fancied that a champion can only lose his primacy in the ring, Wilfred had defended his crown for the third and last time and would never make light welterweight again.

By now it was an open secret in boxing circles that he had formed an almost pathological aversion to serious training. Preferring to burn calories in the premier Latin night spots of New York and San Juan, 'El Radar' was an arrested adolescent whose genius in the squared circle was not mirrored in any other aspect of his life. He could beat fringe world class fighters on talent alone but if he saw Bruce Curry as a convenient stepping stone en route to a world title shot at the higher poundage then Goyo had news for him:

"Curry will knock you out..! You haven't been training. Nobody will fight Curry because he has a punch."

Curry, who had 13 straight wins as a pro, also hailed from a trio of boxing brothers and had lost to Sugar Ray Leonard in the 1976 U.S Olympic trials before making the transition 3 months later. Unpaid records are harder to verify but his given log of 315 - 11 was probably a reasonably accurate representation of a decorated amateur career that included a victory over future all-time great, Mike McCallum. On Friday November 18 at The Garden, Bruce came perilously close to defeating another future all-time great when he floored an ill prepared Benitez twice in the fourth round and again in the fifth. Describing the first knockdown, from a picture perfect left hook that left Wilfred face down in accidental parody of Muslim prayer, Teddy Brenner recalled, "He got off the deck with one leg walking north and the other east. There's no way he should have gotten up and continued. I don't know what carried him through that fight." Echoing the notion that every cloud has a silver lining, the Delphic Cus D'Amato agreed:

"If there was any doubt about his courage, this fight made you take your hat off to him. When he got off that floor, you wouldn't have given two cents for his chances."

Somehow, Benitez recovered well enough to finish the fight on equal terms but the split decision in his favour was hugely controversial. His saving grace had been found in New York's adherence to the antiquated rounds scoring system that did not delineate a boxer's margin of effectiveness in any given round. Under the now universally applied '10 point Must' system, any fighter scoring a knockdown is almost always awarded a 2-point margin on a default basis and 2 knockdowns by the same fighter will generally result in the round being scored 10-7. Under the old system, it made no difference if a fighter battered his opponent from pillar to post in any 3-minute period or simply got his nose in front in a cagey battle of jabs. On that basis, Barney Smith scored 7-3 in the ex-champion's favour whilst Carol Castellano had him squeaking home with a tally of 5-4-1. Referee, Arthur Mercante, turned in an identical score for Curry, perhaps due to his closer proximity to a gruelling slugfest that he described as 'one of the best fights I have ever been in.' As Wilfred waved a large Puerto Rican flag by way of celebration, many in the house expressed their vocal displeasure at a verdict that could not possibly have been rendered had the fight taken place 10 years later. Ultimately, it mattered not. The teenage veteran had escaped with his unbeaten record intact and would live to fight another day.

If Harold Weston represented cause for alarm then Bruce Curry had been tantamount to an air raid siren. Goyo's foreboding prophecy had nearly come to pass and the projection was bleak if his son continued to cut corners in the gym as if right angles were going out of fashion. "He trained about 10 minutes for that fight," reckoned Teddy Brenner, although the more realistic estimate stood at 7 days. When his defensive wizardry failed him, it was now known that Wilfred Benitez had cajones the size of the Soviet Army but balls alone wouldn't beat Pipino Cuevas or Carlos Palomino, the binary kingpins of the welterweight division.

Disgusted with the decision, Curry went back to his adopted hometown of Los Angeles and signed to fight Minoru Sugiya in Tokyo on January 26, 1978 for a reported 10 thousand dollars. Shortly afterwards, he got a call from Madison Square Garden offering him a rematch with Benitez on February 4 for $12, 500. "We were really in a bind," admitted Curry's manager, Jessie Reid. "We were committed to the fight in Japan, where Bruce is something of a hero. And we wanted the rematch with Benitez after the robbery they gave us. We figured we'd just go ahead with both fights." Ignoring protests from the Garden regarding the exclusivity of his services, Curry flew to the Far East and duly destroyed the home fighter in 3 rounds, scoring 5 knockdowns in the process. The next day he took the 10-hour flight back to LA before resting for 24 hours and flying to New York, 6 days before the Benitez encore. Although Sugiya had not extended him unduly, 3 long haul flights in the space of a week hardly constituted the ideal preparation for a fight in which so much was at stake for both parties.

"I know why they fought that bum in Japan," confided Goyo to a journalist. "To build Curry's confidence. After we beat him, he had to be down. It was a smart move on their part. But it won't help him. We are going to put him in a hospital this time."

With Papa Benitez not inclined to take chances, Wilfred was sequestered to a 4-week training camp at altitude in Mexico City where he is said to have sparred over a hundred rounds. Concurring with his father's contention that he had been in woeful shape the first time, he explained, "The first fight was supposed to be with Duran. Then Duran got sick and they said I was fighting Curry instead. I said, 'Curry who..?' And I stopped working. He knocked me down three times. Then I knew who Curry was. This time I have worked very hard. I no play."

Living up to the pre-fight promises, a sharper, more cautious Benitez stayed on the outside and controlled the first 5 rounds against an appreciably flatter version of the man he had encountered 2 months earlier. Conceding that the hectic travel itinerary had worked to his detriment, Curry later admitted, "I just wanted to get it done and go to bed. I should have sent out for coffee." Only for a fleeting moment did Bruce threaten to turn the tide - when he caught Wilfred with a stray left hook, a second and a half after the bell to end Round 7. Bleeding freely from the nose and on the receiving end of a right hand/ left hook/ right uppercut combo, Curry slung a retaliatory sucker punch that seemed to stagger Benitez as referee, Tony Perez, jumped in to separate the two. Scrambling into the ring with almost motherly concern, Goyo's assistant Jaran Manzaret yelled, "Get him...! He's hurt..!" before guiding his man back to the corner.

Smelling salts were allegedly used in the interval but when the action recommenced there was clearly no semblance of a crisis as Wilfred continued to do his thing - jabbing, boxing and unloading in bursts. One thing he didn't do was run. In spite of that fabled ability to avoid punishment like a man emerging bone dry from a shower, Wilfred Benitez never ran. The crux of his defence was founded in the hands and subtle upper body movement as much as the fleet footed speed that he undoubtedly possessed. He wasn't Willie Pep and he wasn't Cassius Clay since neither homage would have satisfied the Latin machismo. Neither would it have satisfied the Garden fans who maintained a rousing chorus of boisterous approval as Wilfred swept the last 2 rounds to take a majority decision. Out of sync with his colleagues, Al Reid gave Curry a draw but perhaps he might also have given Custer a draw at Little Big Horn. Tony Perez and Artie Aidala had seen a different fight and scored for Benitez by margins of 9-1 and 7-3 respectively. The stigma of the previous November had been erased and neither Curry nor his team could scream robbery on this occasion. Nevertheless, when Jesse Reid cashed a thousand dollar expenses cheque at the Garden box office and later discovered a counterfeit $100 bill amongst the readies, he was bound to ask, "Good Lord, what else can they do to us in this town..?"

Before the fight it had been reported in the press that the winner was nailed on to face Roberto Duran in a lucrative non-title affair at MSG on April 27. Goyo begged to differ. "Hold on a minute. We haven't signed any contract to fight Duran. There are still a few things to discuss." The Garden were offering $60,000 (compared with a $100,000 guarantee for Duran) at a contract weight of 143 pounds. Goyo wanted another 40 thousand dollars and 2 extra pounds - unless somebody cared to buy him out of Wilfred's contract entirely:

"I want to sell my kid. All I ask is $150,000, 10 percent of all his future purses and 2 tickets to all of his fights. I say to all of them, 'You put the money in my hand and I put my kid in your hand.' After that, I don't care what you do with my kid. If the new owner wants him to fight Duran at 143 pounds, that is his worry. I want to be like Pontius Pilate... wash my hands of the whole thing."

8/ THE FIX WASN'T IN

People in the business said that Goyo's avowed interest in selling Wilfred's contract stemmed from his addictive passion for 'fast women and slow horses.' In addition to a stable of thoroughbreds, he had a compulsive gambling problem that had placed him in tens of thousands of debt they said. It was a version of events that Teddy Brenner reiterated in his memoir 'Only The Ring Was Square' : 'Gregorio Benitez was in horses. He owned them and played them. And when things went bad, he decided to sell the contract on his son.'

By all available testimony, a none too flattering portrayal emerges of Goyo as a controlling, abusive father who sacrificed the long-term neurological health of his sons in order to facilitate a lifestyle and legacy. It's a portrayal for which one seems to find more corroboration than denial although Yvonne Benitez insists that her father's good character has been sullied by wagging tongues. Goyo had no control over Wilfred's finances and had bought the stable of racehorses with his own money but 'people like to talk' she would tell an interviewer many years later whilst doting on the wreckage of her most famous younger brother. Pressing needs aside, perhaps there were peripheral reasons behind Goyo's desire to relinquish a degree of responsibility in the affairs of a son who had become increasingly ungovernable.

When he should have been training for Randy Shields, a solid contender who demanded an entry level of respect, Benitez was nowhere to be found. "I had every Puerto Rican detective in New York out looking for him," admitted Brenner. Possibly seeking to revert to the childhood he had never been permitted, Wilfred absconded to Disney World where he and a lady friend spent a week of unsanctioned leisure until Goyo tracked him down - a thousand miles from NYC. "I rode all the rides. I rode the submarine, I went into the past," explained the man child when accounting for his absence. That he had become unmanageable - even by the man whose word had previously been held as law - was something Brenner regarded as inevitable. "When you try to do this to an 18-year-old kid who has been disciplined all his life, you're going to get rebellion. I've noticed it since he won the title and people began to pat him on the back and he realised he was an individual. Rebellion set in. Happens all the time in boxing between father and son. Never fails."

Apparently none the worse for his frivolous excursion, Benitez battered Shields into submission on August 25 at Madison Square Garden when the latter declined to answer the bell for the seventh round. In the chief support, soon to be world middleweight king, Vito Antuofermo, won an unpopular decision over the ill fated Willie Classen - prompting a small scale riot in the house. Being Puerto Rican born, Classen (a former heroin addict fighting out of the South Bronx) was the beneficiary of Benitez' fervent supporter's club who greeted the verdict with a hail of bottles and chairs directed towards the ring. 5 fights and 15 months later, Classen died as a result of the injuries he sustained during a 10th round KO loss to Wilford Scypion downstairs at the Felt Forum. Lest he might be considered another statistical tragedy in a subculture laced with 'feel bad' stories. Willie's untimely demise eventually led to a bill which made it mandatory for promoters to have an ambulance present at all fight cards in New York State. In the course of a patchy 16- 7-2 career, he never saw the kind of money that the star of the show would subsequently squander but the value of his accidental martyrdom is incalculable.

After the Shields fight, Goyo sold Wilfred's contract to Jim Jacobs and Bill Cayton for $75,000.[2] A pair of entrepreneurs and fight film collectors with tight links to the legendary Cus D'Amato, Jimmy and Bill had to know they had procured the services of one of the world's best pound for pound fighters at a knockdown price. Over the next 4 years, Benitez would earn an estimated six and a half million dollars under their stewardship although precisely what became of such a veritable fortune is anybody's guess. As lucrative as it proved, the relationship didn't get off to the best of starts when Team Benitez came to stay at D'Amato's fabled house in upstate New York at the tail end of 1978. Jacobs and Cayton had wasted no time in securing their new charge a shot at Carlos Palomino's WBC welterweight title (scheduled for January 14, 1979) and suggested he set up camp at Cus' rather stately home near the Catskill Mountains.

---

[2] "Teddy Brenner offered myself and Mike Jones the Benitez contract. I assumed Benitez's father needed money. I said I would call him the following morning with a decision. We decided to make the deal and I called Brenner who informed me that he had also offered the deal to Jacobs and Cayton who had gotten back to him and had accepted the deal . I often wonder 'what if'..? Like the old song 'What a Difference A Day Makes.' The father had a big gambling problem from what I heard. I don't know the specifics but I wouldn't be surprised if that had a lot to do with it."

-    Dennis Rappaport

In theory it was a good idea but nobody had legislated for what would prove to be a profound clash of cultures in practice. According to author, Peter Heller, Wilfred and his entourage immediately showed themselves to be horrifically uncouth and unacquainted with even the most basic standards of personal hygiene and ablution. Routinely they would spit on the floor and eat with their hands at mealtimes whilst generally turning the civilised ambience of the household on its head. When the other residents complained, D'Amato initially insisted that allowances must be made for people who knew only 'how to cut sugar cane all day and screw their women at night.' But Cus allegedly drew the line when Benitez exhibited an unhealthy libidinous interest in a local 13-year-old girl - explaining that whatever might be deemed acceptable on the Islands could land him dead or in jail in America. The final straw came when D'Amato's live in companion became aware of a lamentable confusion regarding the appropriate use of toilet paper and her expensive monochrome towels. Soon after, the Benitez contingent were sent on their way. "This fellow has a terrible ego. He won't admit that there are some things about boxing that he doesn't know," concluded Cus.

Although the contract included Goyo's retention as a trainer for 10 percent of purses, it was at this point that Emile Griffith entered the equation as an auxiliary coach. An all-time great from the previous era - only 16 months retired - Emile was charged with the task of fine tuning Wilfred's technique and shortening his punches. Inevitably, Goyo's ego was threatened by the presence of a 'sacred cow' on his turf and it's conceivable that he felt a degree of vindication when Benitez' first outing under the new arrangement almost ended in disaster. With the Palomino fight nailed on, Jacobs and Cayton opted to keep their investment busy with a 10 round 'tune up' at The Garden, 2 and a half weeks before Christmas, 1978. His opponent, a dangerous if obscure Guyanese welter by the name of Vernon Lewis, came with nothing to lose and a huge right uppercut that had the favourite out on his feet in the closing seconds of Round 4. His lottery ticket dangling in front of him, Lewis followed up with a two fisted barrage, battering his man from pillar to post for the remainder of the round as John Condon exclaimed, "Benitez has got all kinds of trouble..!" Surviving the onslaught with an equal combination of guts and guile, Wilfred ambled back to his corner with a truculent swagger, shaking his head whilst the old man began furiously massaging his legs in official acknowledgment of a crisis. Relegated to the role of bucket boy, Griffith momentarily entered the ring before immediately retreating back through the ropes as the ring girl performed a vivacious salsa dance.

Prone to lapses in concentration he might have been but there was nothing wrong with the recuperative powers of Benitez who came out for the 5th round as if nothing had happened. The ensuing 18 minutes were tough - one might even say gruelling - but there was no quarrelling with the unanimous decision in the Puerto Rican's favour. Despite the victory, he had looked 'like anything but a strong challenger' in the considered opinion of Steve Cady reporting for the New York Times and that view was endorsed by Lewis, who picked Palomino to beat his conqueror. In the main event, Roberto Duran stopped Monroe Brooks in the 8th round of another welterweight contest, effectively upstaging Wilfred who had hardly shone against second tier opposition. Although Duran was still officially the undisputed World Lightweight Champion, he would vacate the titles within weeks in order to campaign full time at 147, with his sights set on the winner of Palomino - Benítez.

Like Cervantes before him, Palomino could scarcely be regarded as a flash in the pan, having made 7 defences in an era when world titles weren't given out like parking tickets. Mexican born but domiciled in Los Angeles, he had won his laurels at London's Empire Pool in the summer of 1976 at the expense of hometown favourite, John H. Stracey. In the aftermath of a 12th round KO loss for his man, Stracey's promoter Mickey Duff confessed, "It was a voluntary defence… and to be perfectly honest, we picked what we took to be a competitive, saleable but least dangerous opponent for Stracey. We were never more wrong." 2 and a half years later, the handsome moustachioed champion was installed as a 5/2 favourite over an increasingly erratic Benitez whose latest performance was unlikely to have had the Mexican quaking in his boots. In addition to Wilfred's underdog status, there were rumours of turmoil in his camp with Goyo and Griffith at loggerheads on a daily basis. Emile urged caution and advised against trading with Palomino: "Don't go for a knockout. Palomino is a dangerous one punch fighter. He punches over punches. Keep your hands up and fight to go the distance. Be sharp. If you listen to me you will win." Goyo dismissed the safety first counselling and insisted that the legend's input had little value.

"All Griffith does is tell him about how it was when he was champion. Wilfred doesn't listen to him. He only listens to me."

Emile had boxed more world championship rounds than any fighter in history but was non-confrontational by nature and sought to keep the peace by largely avoiding Papa Benitez outside of training hours. At the very least Wilfred would have hometown advantage at the Hiram Bithorn Stadium and had been more active than the champion who would be making his first ring appearance in seven and a half months. At some point during his previous defence - a 15 round points win over Armando Muniz at the Olympic Auditorium- Carlos had broken his left hand thus leading to the hiatus. In compensation for lost earnings, he would net $465, 000 to risk his title in Benitez' back yard, which was not only a career highest payday but a record for the welterweight division. The challenger's end was 90 grand but that figure would be dwarfed by the financial inducements on offer if he beat Carlos.

Seemingly in deep contemplation of such life changing revenue, Benítez stood in a catatonic trance as he stared across the ring at Palomino on a sunny Sunday afternoon in San Juan. Although never aesthetically out of shape, his body looked exceptionally chiselled with a closer than usual haircut lending an extra sense of purpose to his visage. He wore white shorts trimmed with purple, perhaps desiring not to attract the sun. According to Howard Cosell, it was 87 degrees in the arena - approximating a 'hot sultry breeze' as per the iconic broadcaster's description. Attired in quintessentially 1970s green velvet trunks, Palomino loitered impassively in the blue corner, visibly unperturbed by what Cosell called 'the hostility of the crowd.'

For 3 rounds, Benítez adhered perfectly to the Griffith blueprint of counterpunching from ring centre, making full use of his educated left jab. Then, in Round 4, the champion began to find his range, finally connecting with

59

a few solid right hands and left hooks to the body after a 9-minute scouting report. For much of the fifth round, Wilfred dazzled his adversary with beautiful boxing and fluid combination punching before getting nailed with a big overhand right that seemed to put a dip in his knees, 10 seconds before the bell. Back in the corner, Carlos told manager, Jackie McCoy, that he was ready to step up the pace and take the kid out but any hope that the action had turned in his favour was scuppered as Benítez won the sixth with a mixture of sharpshooting and equal trading. Explaining his inability to turn the screw, Palomino would later say, "I don't know if it was the heat or the long layoff or what but I couldn't move the way I wanted to. I was slow. I could only throw one punch at a time; there were no combinations."

It was Benítez who appeared to rock the champion in Round 7, although the latter never stopped coming forward in an effort to impose himself on an increasingly frustrating (albeit well paid) assignment. The ninth round was the best of the fight, with the combatants exchanging toe to toe for much of the 3 minutes but it was Benítez who got the best of things and was evidently starting to believe that Palomino couldn't hurt him. The title continued to slip away from the soon to be ex-champion in rounds 10 through 13. Every session was closely contested but with the challenger maintaining a constant edge and even his near misses being greeted with vociferous applause from an undivided crowd. There was a hint of desperation in Palominos work in the penultimate round - having been told by McCoy that only a knockout could save his championship as things stood. Overflowing with hubris, Wilfred deliberately retreated to the ropes for the last 30 seconds and gave an Houdini like display of damage limitation before working Carlos over as if he might have been a floor to ceiling ball with facial hair.

It was all over bar the shouting as the fighters prepared to come out for the fifteenth round and the sun began to set - throwing shade on what had previously been a bright coloured affair. Getting back on his jab for the last 180 seconds, Benítez continued to thwart much of Palomino's offence as the fans chanted his name in staccato syllables by way of premature celebration. When the bell rang, an attempt to hug his opponent was scuppered by the rush of handlers and friends who hoisted their hero skywards as they awaited the official decision.

Harry Gibbs, one of Great Britain's premier officials had scored for Benítez by a margin of 146 - 143. Then came the controversy. Zach Clayton, a resident of Philadelphia immortalised by his role as third man in the historic Ali - Foreman fight, had the champion 3 points clear with a total of 145 - 142. By the account of Michael Katz, representing the New York Times, 'the anger of the crowd could be measured by the debris suddenly flying through the air.' Prompted by a colleague from Sports Illustrated, Katz scurried to the safety of the third base dugout in anticipation of a full scale riot before the referee Jay Edson's card was announced:

'EL REFEREE, JAY EDSON, VOTA CIENTO CUARENTA Y TRES - CIENTO CAURENTA Y OCHO… Y EL NUEVO CAMPEON… WILFREDO BENÍTEZ…!

Then came the scenes of jubilation. Asked if he was surprised by the split verdict during a post-fight interview on the ring apron amid a carnival atmosphere,

61

Wilfred told Cosell, "I won the fight and I don't care about the decision. They gave a split decision because he is a great fighter and they didn't want him to lose too bad.."

Promoter, Bob Arum, had a more sinister theory involving the machinations of his natural enemy, Don King. "Nobody in their right mind could have scored that fight for Palomino. I know Palomino. He was a great champion but you watched that fight and I watched that fight and there is no doubt that Benítez won it. We heard rumours that Zach Clayton was under the influence of Don King and Bill Daly (King's Puerto Rican representative) and they wanted Palomino to win because Benítez has the option for Top Rank and Palomino didn't."

Responding to the accusation, Clayton denied he was in King's pocket and asked, "If we're such good friends, how come he's never given me a fight to work..?" Oddly, he also told Katz that the sun had been in his eyes throughout much of the fight and might conceivably have impaired his view of the proceedings. 'Honest' Bill Daly, as he was known in American fight circles, also refuted any charge of unethical bias:

"I was sitting in the first row, rooting for Benítez all the way. I sure wish I could own all the referees - that would be some business."

9/ ALL QUIET ON THE WESTON FRONT

4 weeks after Benítez became a double world champ, Jay Edson had another high profile assignment at the Miami Beach Convention Centre. On this occasion, his scorecard wasn't needed as the rising star, Sugar Ray Leonard, stopped Canadian middleweight champion, Fernand Marcotte, in the eighth round of a nationally televised main event that was blacked out in the local area to protect the live gate. Common practice though it was, the promoter should not have worried unduly. Having won the hearts of mainstream America when he captured Olympic Gold not 3 years earlier with a picture of his baby son taped to his sock, Leonard kept the turnstiles moving wherever he went. Like a pocket sized version of Muhammad Ali with the controversy expunged, his dazzling smile and boardroom eloquence - in addition to exceptional skills - had made him a huge box office attraction. The diehards balked at the temerity with which he had stolen the 'nom de guerre' of boxing's most sacred deity - Sugar Ray Robinson - but any suggestions that the new Sugar Ray was a pure media creation were demonstrably unfair. 19 fights into an already lucrative pro career (earning 5 times more for his debut than Benitez received for his first world title fight) he could count the likes of Armando Muniz, Randy Shields and Floyd Mayweather Sr. amongst his victims. By any modern filter, he was coming up the hard way, albeit with maximum exposure and remuneration.

The tough and seasoned Marcotte couldn't cope with the speed and offensive variety of his naturally smaller opponent and did well to survive as long as he did before a left uppercut/ right hook couplet put paid to his dogged resistance at 2.33 of Round 8. "Welterweight's no problem," Leonard told Dick Enberg in his post-fight address, "But I'm quite sure, in the near future, I'll be a middleweight for 1 million dollars..!"

In spite of his premature allusion, it seemed more likely that the Palmer Park prodigy was on a collision course with either Benitez or his WBA counterpart, Pipino Cuevas, a bone breaking puncher from Mexico City. Add Duran and a streaking knockout specialist from Detroit by the name of Thomas Hearns and the welterweight class looked poised to usurp the heavyweights as boxing's glamour division. The great Ali was nearing the end of the road and the search was on for a new banner star.

With such career defining match ups on the horizon, it's conceivable that Wilfred struggled to get up for the more mundane obligation of a Harold Weston rematch. Since inflicting the sole blemish on Benitez's record, Weston had subsequently been stopped by Cuevas in 9 rounds of a world title challenge at the Olympic Auditorium, the previous year. After being badly rocked in the opening two rounds, an uncharacteristically aggressive Weston was competitive thereafter until a relentless assault from the champion turned his legs to rubber in the conclusive session. Despite trailing on all cards and sustaining a broken jaw, the prize-fighter's capacity for self delusion did not desert Harold when he explained, "I didn't know my jaw was broken. Had I known, I would have continued and stopped Cuevas. At the end of the ninth round, Cuevas' mouthpiece was out and he was gasping for air." Afforded the relative dignity of a corner retirement in his first TKO loss, Weston lived to fight another day.[3]

---

[3] In an interview in 2011, Weston claimed that his jaw was never broken after all.

When that day came, on March 25, 1979 at Hiram Bithorn Stadium, the temperature was 'brutally hot' in the challenger's estimation - "I came into the ring first and was immediately sent to a corner in the sun." Absent from the champion's corner was his father, who had chosen to distance himself from the chaos of Wilfred's life and the lack of vocational focus the came with it. Although brother Gregorio was his nominal chief second, Benitez had essentially taken to training himself and had only put in 3 weeks of anything resembling hard graft for his first title defence at 147. At this point, Emile Griffith had also flown the coop, leaving the WBC King entirely bereft of senior counsel when the first bell rang.

Adhering to the same blueprint he had pursued unsuccessfully against Cuevas - the one which states the challenger must rip the title away - Weston pressured Benitez from the off and was conceivably ahead after 5 rounds. Sporting minor abrasions over both eyes, Benitez finally imposed himself in the sixth, backing Weston to the ropes and unloading with both hands. His ebony skin almost blending with the shade in Wilfred's corner, Weston came back hard in Round 8, dispelling any suspicion that the heat was starting to get to him. Whilst the mid rounds unfolded, Goyo was reportedly accosted at a nearby racetrack by an associate who pressed a radio to his ear and told him that Wilfred was losing the fight. Galvanised into immediate action, he dashed from the track and headed for the stadium, arriving at the end of the 9th round in time to read the riot act. Jumping into the corner and slapping his son's face, he yelled, "What's the matter with you..? Get out there and kill that guy..!"

It was unclear if Benitez was aided or hampered by the intrusive pep talk but Goyo was still unhappy at the end of the eleventh and saw fit to muscle in once more. "This fight is not going well, "he insisted, emphasising his point with two more slaps for good measure. The incongruous appearance of his burgundy red sweatshirt seemed to lend a comic aspect to what was otherwise a scene straight out of 'Rocky.' Like Rocky, Wilfred came on strong in the twelfth and staggered Weston with a left hook and a looping right hand before battering him into a neutral corner to seal his biggest round of the fight. Refusing to leave the helm, Goyo furiously massaged Wilfred's calf muscles and showered him with water from a plastic bottle as he sent his son out for Round 13. If he has gotten a bad rap thus far then let it serve as evidence of genuine fatherly love, tunnelling under the walls of arrogant self-interest.

Weston never stopped trying to force the fight in the last 9 minutes but Benitez was fresher having paced himself better in the early going. The unanimous decision in his favour was not controversial barring the ludicrously wide card of referee, Richard Steele, who had scored for the champion by an effective margin of 12 rounds to 1, with 2 rounds even. In the new decade, Steele would become the most recognisable third man in world boxing - alongside Mills Lane - and would occasionally be accused of bias towards Don King fighters but he had no obvious motive to sabotage a fellow American. Although Harold conceded in the immediate aftermath that Benitez had clearly won the fight, it was apparent in an interview conducted many years later that he had changed his mind: "I would have made $1,000,000 against Leonard had I grabbed the title. The crowd was rough but I know I won that fight. You know that the two Puerto Rican judges had me losing by only 1 and 2 points, in Puerto Rico no less. But the

American referee gave me only one round the whole fight."

Britain's Dave 'Boy' Green had been ringside for the event, labouring under the misapprehension that he would meet the winner in Monte Carlo on May 26. ABC announced the voluntary defence as a done deal but when Jimmy Jacobs received a call from Ray Leonard's attorney, Mike Trainer, Green suddenly found himself on the back burner as negotiations for a super fight were set in motion. Trainer flew to New York and met with Jacobs at his Midtown apartment where the two spent 4 hours embroiled in a civilised battle for primacy and leverage. The biggest single sticking point was Trainer's demand for purse parity. "Wilfred is not an opponent," Jacobs reminded him. "He is the world champion who has never been beaten and he has to be paid more than the challenger."

"Ray is providing nearly 8 times the money Wilfred ever made on a fight," countered Trainer.[4]The Silver Spring lawyer, who by his own admission had known nothing about the business of boxing 3 years earlier, estimated the fight's worth at $2.2 million. Jacobs conceded that he would agree to a 50/50 split if the fight were held in Puerto Rico or New York where Benitez would enjoy the trappings of hometown advantage. Trainer vetoed both locations but eventually offered the champion an extra $100, 000 if the fight were staged at a neutral site, meaning anywhere besides Puerto Rico, NY or Washington. With the record breaking purses agreed - for a non-heavyweight title fight - they then took the package

---

[4] Benitez had reportedly earned $140,000 for the Weston rematch, his biggest purse to date.

to Bob Arum who wasn't immediately convinced that both parties hadn't priced themselves out. "I looked at them like they were crazy," he remembered.

Without asking either manager to compromise their demands, Arum negotiated with ABC whilst giving the impression that he was also in serious talks with NBC and CBS. By his own admission, it was a smokescreen. "I knew that NBC and CBS were not going to come up with what I needed. They were hot for the fight but not at this money. ABC didn't want to lose this fight. It had built up Leonard, I had to give the impression there was fierce competition." Avoiding any substantive discussions with the rival networks, for fear they would drop out, Bob maintained the charade for 2 months before accepting ABC's offer of $1.9 million. From there, he sold the fight to Caesars Palace for $500,000 and picked up a further $150,000 for foreign rights. With $2.55 million in revenues set against $2.2 million in purses, the promoter stood to make around a quarter of a million dollars after expenses. Initially, the date was set for Saturday December 1, before being moved back 24 hours to Friday November 30 at the Caesars Sports Pavilion in Las Vegas.

Given Wilfred's lackadaisical training habits, the saving grace of his career to date had been relatively constant activity. Allowing him to gather dust for the 8 months that separated the Weston and Leonard engagements was not the smartest move on the part of his brain trust - particularly in an era when it was still commonplace for world champions to keep busy in non-title bouts. Leonard, in perfect contrast, fought half a dozen times between the trouncing of Marcotte and his first world title challenge - with 3 of those outings coming after the Benitez fight had been signed. On June 24, the capable but outgunned Tony Chiaverini was unable to answer the bell for the fifth round due to the sound thrashing he had received up to that point. As the tough Kansas City southpaw was bludgeoned into submission, a distinction was fast emerging. Although he was being marketed as a more media friendly Ali in miniature, a ruthless, flat footed banger clearly lurked behind the style and profile. 7 weeks later, NABF Welterweight Champion Pete Ranzany was stopped in four as boxing's heir apparent grabbed his first professional title. "Like I said a long time ago, I'm gonna' be the champ," proclaimed Leonard in the aftermath. "I got half of the belt, I want the other half from Benitez.

If the new Sugar Ray had looked impressive in disposing of Chaverini and Ranzany, then his one round annihilation of Andy 'The Hawk' Price in late September was positively chilling. In the 21st century, it seems unthinkable that a fighter on the verge of the richest welterweight title challenge in history would risk meeting a contender of Price's quality, 8 weeks prior to the big one. It seems equally unthinkable that a heavyweight main event as compelling as Larry Holmes vs Earnie Shavers would be supported by an undercard featuring Sugar Ray Leonard, Roberto Duran and Wilfredo Gomez. Those who were lucky enough to be present outdoors at Caesars Palace got to see the least of Leonard as he hurt his man early before backing him to the ropes and unloading with a blistering volley of punches from which Price had no choice but to fall. Andy had beaten Cuevas and Palomino but was made to resemble the proverbial 'Mexican road-sweeper' by the WBC's No. 2 ranked contender who pocketed $300, 000 for an easy night's work.

Whilst Leonard was as sharp as a tungsten needle, familiar noises emanated from the champion's camp regarding his customary aversion to hard work and sacrifice. Goyo was sufficiently dismayed to put his name to an article in Ring Magazine entitled, 'Why Benitez Will Lose His Title.'

"Both my wife and I are very disgusted with Wilfred. Even if they gave me $200,000 to work in the corner, I would not. He has not listened to anything I have told him; he would rather be out somewhere - anywhere - other than the gym. I have told him many times that Leonard will be in top shape and in top form, and that Leonard will beat him if he doesn't train."

10/ SUGAR SMACK

It soon became apparent that one could add the subtle art of the psychologist to Goyo's impressive list of competences. The article had been a ploy, he claimed, intended to make his son work harder. "If I tell him he's going to win, Wilfred won't work hard. Now I think nobody can beat him. He's in the best shape of all time." Jim Jacobs endorsed the father's reverse psychology. "I have to convince Wilfred to build this guy up so when he beats him he'll be recognised as a great fighter." The oddsmakers, who deal in probability rather than psychology, installed the challenger as a 3-1 favourite - prompting both father and manager to lump 10 thousand dollars on their man. By way of reassurance, Wilfred dismissed the calculations of the Las Vegas gambling fraternity.

"I don't care if he's favoured. I will knock him out. He won't take my punch. He's just a boxer. I'm the 'Bible of Boxing.' He's a great boxer but this time he's fighting with the champion."

Any allusions to the champion's erratic form were met with a caveat from Jacobs: "When Wilfred fights an ordinary fighter, he looks ordinary. (But) He's had better fights in his father's gymnasium in Puerto Rico than Leonard has had in the ring." Significant perhaps was that Leonard - for all his brilliance - had never been beyond 10 rounds whilst Benitez had completed the championship distance on four previous occasions. Teddy Brenner certainly thought so. "If it goes 15 rounds, there's no question Benitez will win. Leonard has to stop him." It would prove to be an ironic prediction.

Although he would eventually claim not to have trained for the fight, Wilfred raised eyebrows when he showed up late for the weigh in and came in surprisingly light at 144 pounds. [5]Ordinarily, it might have pointed to overtraining or malnourishment but the 'Bible of boxing' was a law unto himself and appeared to be doing something right regardless. At 21 years of age, he was undefeated in 39 professional fights - with the tie against Weston being the singular blot on the landscape.

Leonard, 2 years older at 23, was unbeaten in 25 starts with 16 of those wins coming via the knockout route. It was a mouth-watering match up for the connoisseurs - the like of which contemporary fans on the internet refer to as 'boxing porn.' And echoing the adult analogy, the old guru Cus D'Amato wondered if Sugar Ray could take it in the same manner that he was clearly able to dish it out. "He has never been hit as he is going to be hit in this fight. He's going to know what it is to fight a consummate professional."

On the latter account one might have begged to differ. Marvin Hagler, who would finally receive his overdue tilt at the Undisputed Middleweight Crown in the co - feature, was a consummate professional. Wilfred Benitez was an enigmatic and reluctant genius, dragging his heels through the only life he had ever known.

---

[5] According to boxing historian, Steve Compton, the late Steve Lott refuted the oft cited version of events that Benitez was ill prepared for the Leonard fight: "He was Benitez' minder when Jacobs and Cayton managed him. He said the stories that Benitez trained for only a week or two for Leonard were bullshit. He said he was with him the whole time and he had trained hard and had a normal camp for that fight."

In accordance with protocol, Leonard was first to enter the ring, wearing a white satin robe that made him appear angelic. Celestial even. Seeking to take psychological possession of the 20-foot square domain, he performed an Ali shuffle followed by a 'shoeshine' combo of rapid fire uppercuts before banging his gloves down on the outstretched palms of assistant trainer, Janks Morton. When the champion arrived, sporting a Persian blue silk gown trimmed with white, the fighters gravitated towards one another and locked eyes in ring centre. The initial stare down - eventually broken off by Leonard with a wink - served as a prelude to the more intimate, nose to nose face off that ensued several seconds later. Benitez, now denuded of robe and the green plastic belt that denoted his supremacy, tilted his head askance and puffed out his chest whilst the challenger stood firm and catatonic for 20 odd seconds. Ali - Sugar Ray's precursor - was acknowledged as the pioneer of the now time honoured ritual of self assertion but never before had it so perfectly encapsulated the majestic narcissism of exceptional prize-fighters in their pomp. Significantly or not, Leonard was the first to look away and walk back to his corner. Perhaps he had seen what he needed to see.

As Chuck Hull made the introductions it became apparent that the crowd was evenly divided in terms of loyalty, at least judging by the decibels that greeted each fighter's name. The Golden Boy Heir Apparent vs the Latin American Idol with no hyperbole required in an age that still ranked substance over style. Leonard won the first round by virtue of a pair of left hooks that amounted to the difference in an otherwise cagey battle of jabs. Not dancing, he had clearly resolved to take it to Benitez in accordance with the unwritten rule that places the burden of proof on the challenger. "Don't look for the right hand, work into it..!" barked Angelo Dundee in Leonard's corner during the interval. "Don't load up... BOX... You're the pro, he's nuthin'...!" Angie didn't do the spade work in camp but as a master of strategy and kidology, he had the gravitas that Goyo craved.

Round 2 was a feinting contest with more damage done to the air than either protagonist before a stiff left jab dumped Benitez on the seat of his blue velvet trunks at the end of the third. Rising from the 'flash knockdown' with the alacrity of the blow that floored him, the champion grinned and then nodded with a mixture of hubris and embarrassment. Conceivably, he was already 4 points adrift in a chess game that favoured the bigger commercial animal in the storied Mecca of Chance. The fourth round saw no clear advantage to either man as Leonard continued to score with a rapier jab but missed with a slew of chopping right hands and left hooks. ("No one, I mean NO ONE can make me miss punches like that," he would say after the fight.) But whilst the proficiency of his Houdini act was well documented Benitez simply wasn't throwing enough punches to win rounds against a media darling with a perceptible edge in hand speed.

Wilfred arguably had the best of Round 5 but fortune, physics and biology conspired against him in the next frame when an accidental clash of heads opened a cut on his forehead. With the blood cascading freely into his eyes and mouth, the champion responded with a spirited 2 fisted attack, causing Leonard to stand and trade for the time in the fight. As Goyo dabbed at the source of flowing claret with a white towel in between rounds, his youngest son smiled like a truculent adolescent made to stand in front of the class for disruptive behaviour. Based on any moderately upbeat expectations, things were not going well.

The seventh and eighth were also Leonard rounds in which he started to find the range for the right uppercut and left hook more frequently. With the fight more than half over, the deficit was beginning to look unassailable as a mocked up 'Roman' ring girl brandished her numerical update for those who struggled with arithmetic. The pro Benitez contingent chanted 'WILFRED' in Round 9 which seemed to lift their hero - although he might only have shared the spoils in a torrid session that saw both men score with hurtful shots to head and body. The tenth belonged to the champion as he landed a jolting straight left counter and several right hands but the tide turned again in Round 11 as Benitez was staggered by a left hook and lost his mouthpiece during the follow up barrage. Despite being in unchartered territory, Leonard appeared the fresher of the two and was almost certainly up on the scorecards. "Don't go to sleep, please...!" urged Dundee at end of the twelfth. "You can go 9 minutes, can't you..? You can go all night long for a title..!"

Responding in the affirmative, Sugar Ray clearly won Round 13 whilst Benitez seemed content merely to stay with his man, like a sparring partner on daily rate. His slippery defiance acknowledged, the WBC champion hardly resembled a man who would walk through hell fire to retain his precious laurels. The penultimate round followed the established pattern of what had been an absorbing affair rather than a thriller but Angelo Dundee had been around too long to count his chickens:

"THIS FIGHT IS VERY CLOSE - YOU GOTTA' FIGHT LIKE AN ANIMAL...! DON'T BACK UP, TAKE IT TO HIM..!"

Such urgency would have been more pertinent in the opposite corner but the passionate histrionics that had characterised Goyo's performance during the Weston rematch were strangely absent. Perhaps a part of him wanted to see his pre-fight prediction validated. With Leonard under orders, both fighters abandoned the more technical aspects of the sweet science in the fifteenth round and a slugfest finally ensued. Winging savagely - as if the gravity of the situation had suddenly dawned on him - Benitez gave as good as he got until a left hook caused him to topple onto all fours with 25 seconds left on the clock. Once again, he scarcely took a count but the unsteady gait with which he ambled to a neutral corner was reminiscent of the Bruce Curry debacle 2 years earlier. Symbolically, the previously congealed cut on his crown was bleeding afresh as Carlos Padilla waved the fight on.

Ever the ruthless finisher, Leonard pinned Benitez in the corner and landed a right hand / left hook before missing with a left uppercut and another right hand only for Padilla to stop the fight with 6 seconds remaining. It would have been a hugely controversial call had the contest been evenly balanced, but with the challenger ahead by 7, 4 and 2 points respectively on the official scoresheets, it was ultimately academic. Certainly there was no protest from the deposed champion as he immediately walked over to his jubilant conqueror and embraced him warmly. Perhaps the 7-figure compensation for his first reversal in 40 professional fights went some way towards sugaring the pill.

In his post-fight interview with Howard Cosell, Leonard extended 'a special prayer and consolation to the family of Willie Classen' who had died 7 days earlier for a pittance of pay in pursuit of the same dream. Contrary to the standard rumours of skulduggery, some said the spectre of Willie's tragic demise was in the back of Padilla's mind when he stopped the fight. Not inclined to sour grapes, Jim Jacobs supported the referee's intervention. "I'm glad he stopped the fight. I didn't want the fighter to get hurt." Sporting a visible gash and a swollen left thumb at the press conference, Benitez graciously conceded:

"I have no excuses. He won easy, you know..? He'll win a lot of fights, like I do when I was champion... He's a great challenger. He became a champion beating me. I want to give him a good luck and God bless him."

Frankie 'The Terror' Benitez in his prime.

Wilfred and Goyo in the glory years.

Benitez v Cervantes, March 6 1976

Benitez outpoints Emiliano Villa in first defence of WBA light-
welterweight title. May 31 1976

'Eye of the tiger' – Benitez v Leonard, November 30 1979, Las Vegas

Wilfred enjoys the trappings of 'Sin City' (1982)

(Photo Credit; Linda Platt.

'El Radar' as captured by Linda Platt in the early 1980s

With Wilfredo Gomez and Lupe Pintor ahead of 'The Carnival of Champions'

'The morning after', with mother, Clara.

Wilfred and his wife Elizabeth Alonso with baby daughter
Isabel. 1983

Prefight with Ray Chavez Guerrero 1977.

Staring down the 'Motor City Cobra' December 1982.

Father and Son work the mitts.

Jumping for joy after becoming the fifth man in history to win world titles in 3 weight classes.

May 23 1981.

Taking it on the chin from Palomino. January 14 1979

Beating Duran at his own game. January 30 1982.

With Marvin Hagler at the International Boxing Hall of Fame
Ceremony, June 1996

Wilfred pictured recently in Chicago with sister, Yvonne and friends.

11/ THIRD TIME'S A CHARM

'Irish' Johnny Turner - the designated obstacle on the first leg of the Benitez comeback trail - had reason to regard himself as a viable nemesis. Having beaten a 14-year-old Wilfred in a 1973 amateur meet, Turner rubbed salt in the wound when he stopped the remnants of brother Frankie 5 years later at Madison Square Garden. On the night in question, it seems that the lanky New Yorker was originally slated to face Wilfred until Goyo pulled him out 3 days before the show and brought Frankie in as a substitute. Whatever the old man's reasoning, there was clearly no love lost between the two factions. "I was supposed to fight Wilfred in May, 1978 at Madison Square Garden but he chickened out and they sent his brother Frankie to fight for him," claimed Turner. "So I made Frankie pay for that. I beat him up and I knocked him out. I already beat Wilfred in 1973 and I'll do it again."

The overdue rematch took place on March 16, 1980 at the Jai- Alai Fronton Arena in Miami where it became readily apparent that Turner would struggle to fulfil his prediction without the aid of a time machine. Weighing in at a solid 150 pounds and wearing red trunks with a white trim, Benitez set his stall out early - flooring Turner with a counter left hook before a full minute had elapsed. Thereafter, the crowd witnessed a workmanlike beatdown as the dogged Brooklynite was rocked several times en route to a 9th round stoppage, his features obscured by crisscrossing rivulets of blood when the ringside doctor stopped the fight. Although at least one of the cuts was caused by an accidental clash of heads in the previous round, Turner had been soundly outclassed by an altogether different animal to the skinny adolescent he had bested 7 years earlier. Whilst naturally craving a rematch with Leonard, Wilfred looked well at the higher poundage and his team were already eyeing a shot at WBC light middleweight champion, Maurice Hope. Feeling that their charge had failed to shine since Palomino, Jacobs and Cayton brought back Emile Griffith whose high octave pearls of wisdom could be heard throughout the CBS Sunday afternoon broadcast. Angelo Dundee, working as a ringside analyst for the network was sufficiently impressed to remark, "Benitez is a great fighter. He has everything out there."

With Hope tied into a rematch with former champion, Rocky Mattioli, in July, Jacobs and Cayton initially pressed for Benitez to meet the winner in September - offering a $50,000 step aside fee to No.1 contender, Carlos Herrera, in a bid to make it happen. When that offer was rebuffed, they opted to keep their man busy in a 10-rounder vs former Sugar Ray Leonard victim, Tony Chiaverini, in Las Vegas on August 1. Chiaverini, coming off 7 straight wins since his drubbing at the hands of Leonard, held a top ten ranking with the WBC at 154 and nursed hopes of a world title shot if he could get past Benitez. Seeking to rebuild in the aftermath of the Sugarman loss he had hooked up with Angelo Dundee and had yet to put a foot wrong under his tutelage. Nonetheless, Angelo - the sole architect of Benitez' downfall in a professional ring - had a maxim for those who thought him a miracle worker. "I'm only as good as the guy on the stool," he explained with due modesty.

As it happened, the guy on the stool was mercifully prevented from getting off that stool at the beginning of the 9th round, due to the steady pummelling he had received in the preceding 24 minutes. Benitez, weighting a career heaviest 155 pounds, struggled to miss the aggressive marauding southpaw with lead rights and left hooks even when lingering on the ropes for extended periods. While lauded for his defensive wizardry, Wilfred didn't have the safety first mindset of latter day 'untouchables' like Pernell Whitaker and Floyd Mayweather Jnr. having forged his fighting ethos in the schoolyard scraps of his childhood. And so, sportingly, he afforded Chiaverini the chance to make a go of things on the inside, albeit to no avail. Providing a sense of relatable drama for viewers of NBC's 'Friday Night Fights' was Chiaverini's wife at ringside who kept up a steady stream of vocal encouragement juxtaposed with visible signs of dismay when her man absorbed 'El Radar's heavier artillery. On the subject of branding, the winner revealed his preferred new moniker to Ferdie Pacheco in the postscript:

"I WANT ROBERTO DURAN...! ROBERTO DURAN, HE'S AFRAID OF ME.. I AM 'THE DRAGON'..!"

6 weeks earlier, Duran had sensationally dethroned Leonard in an epic slugfest in Montreal and 24 hours later in Detroit, Thomas Hearns would annihilate Pipino Cuevas in 2 rounds to annexe the WBA Welterweight crown. Alluding to Benitez' filled out 21-year-old frame, the 'Fight Doctor' asked if he could still make 147 without forfeiting his burgeoning man strength...? In charming broken English he responded, "If I train hard.. If I have more 'dedicate' with boxing and training, I think I'm not gonna' have no problem to 'became' champion again."

When he closed out the year with a 10 round points win over Pete Ranzany on December 12 in Sacramento,

California, Wilfred weighed 150 and a quarter. The show was promoted by the imminently notorious Muhammad Ali Professional Sports group - contrived by a man who said his name was Harold Smith - and the winner had been promised a shot at Tommy Hearns, on a blockbuster card set for Madison Square Garden on February 23, 1981. Fighting in his hometown, Ranzany put in a gallant shift but came up against a breathtakingly sharp Benitez who produced one of his best performances. The head movement that had always been his trademark seemed to have leapfrogged into the realm of telepathy as 'Pistol Pete' consistently struggled to find the target despite a frenetic work rate.

Adding to the Californian beanpole's logistical problems was the unerring accuracy with which Benitez landed his own combinations, the effortless fluidity complementing his aqua blue shorts.

Winking at Don Dunphy's verbal spar mate and recently crowned WBA light welterweight champion, Aaron Pryor, at the start of Round 5, Benitez nailed Ranzany with an overhand right and a subsequent volley of left hooks that had him on rubbery legs. For a split second, the possibility of a stoppage loomed but Pete was made of stern stuff and battled back gamely. "Ranzany comes to fight," remarked Pryor. "He gets hit with those big hard punches and comes right back." The ninth round was poetry in motion as Benitez slipped and jerked his handsome physiognomy out of harm's way with casual ease before shaking his man with a left hook/ right hand shortly before the bell. "I think the bell saved him that round. I think he's hurt," opined Aaron Pryor.

"Benitez is hitting harder than he's hit in a long time," proclaimed Dunphy as Wilfred connected with 3 left hooks at the start of the tenth. "He's taking target practice with Ranzany now." Although the Puerto Rican favourite was almost certainly ahead on the cards, Ranzany had scarcely taken a backward step in "..one of the best fights I've seen in a long time," according to the most senior of American fight announcers. When the crowd booed the unanimous decision in Benitez' favour it owed much to geographical bias but the object of their myopic affection knew the score: "He's a very difficult man to hit. One second he is there and, the next second, he is gone. He kept me off balance and I couldn't put anything together." If Ranzany sought consolation in defeat then perhaps there was an upside to avoiding a date with the murderous punching Hearns, regardless of fiscal incentive. As it turned out, Benitez wouldn't face Hearns either - at least not on the scheduled date of February 23.

Harold Smith - the man who planned to take over boxing with the simple strategy of overpaying marquee fighters with embezzled funds - went missing in late January amid a storm of allegations that his exorbitant budget (over $20 million) had been siphoned from the coffers of the Wells Fargo Bank in Beverly Hills. With the main man missing in action, the Garden mega show - also set to feature Eddie Mustafa Muhammad, Aaron Pryor, Matthew Saad Muhammad, Wilfredo Gomez, and a non-title heavyweight clash between Gerry Cooney and Ken Norton - was officially scrapped on February 6, less than 3 weeks before the crystallisation of Smith's cocaine fuelled dream. Muhammad Ali, who had merely lent to his name to the enterprise, remained untarnished by the subsequent scandal while Smith (real name Ross Fields) was arrested in Los Angeles, 10 weeks after his disappearance and sentenced to 10 years imprisonment the following year. Given that none of the estimated $21.3

million of misappropriated readies was ever recovered, one might have considered it an occupational hazard.

With Wilfred's immediate future cast into uncertainty, Bob Arum made a bid to salvage the Hearns fight in the wake of the MAPS collapse. Under Smith's illegally sponsored largesse Benitez had been set to earn $1 million but Arum is believed to have pitched somewhere in the region of 6 to 7 hundred thousand dollars. In an interview with Michael Katz for the New York Times, Jim Jacobs thanked the promoter for his 'generous offer' whilst stating that it was 'a quarter million short' of incurring his fighter's signature. As a consequence, he revealed, Benitez would challenge for Maurice Hope's WBC light middleweight title in the Spring as previously mooted - for half a million less than Arum was offering to fight Hearns. Jacobs' sound reasoning in this regard was based on the fight game's most fundamental equation that pits risk against reward:

"Why would we take less to fight Hope than to fight Hearns..? The answer is in 2 words: 10 years. That's the difference between fighting an undefeated 22-year-old and a 32 year old. There is a difference between Thomas Hearns and Maurice Hope. And Wilfred would be going for his third world title. Not since Henry Armstrong has anyone won three world titles."

According to the Ring Record Book, Hope was actually 29 but there was no denying that the British / Antiguan southpaw constituted a decidedly less dangerous assignment than the Detroit City 'Hitman' who had iced 27 of his 29 professional victims at the time of writing. And while posterity didn't pay the bills, in context of the era, Benitez stood on the verge of a truly remarkable feat

- only preceded by a quartet of fistic immortals named Fitzsimmons, Ross, Canzoneri and Armstrong. At the still tender age of 22, he would also boast the distinction of being boxing's youngest triple champ if the bookies had done their sums correctly. Hearns - himself on a collision course with Sugar Ray Leonard since the latter had avenged his loss to Duran - would keep until the uneasy bedfellows, risk and reward, had aligned themselves more agreeably.

If Maurice Hope represented the easier option at a fair price then he was certainly no patsy. A Londoner since the age of 10, as part of the Windrush generation, the 1972 Olympian had trodden a traditional path to the top - winning British, Commonwealth and European titles at 10st before wresting the WBC strap from Mattioli in San Remo in March, 1979. Since then he had made 3 successful defences (vs Mike Baker, Mattioli and Carlos Herrera) and would earn a career highest payday of $250, 000 for putting his belt on the line at Caesars Palace on May 23. Introverted to a fault, he remained a fiercely proud warrior who, despite a controversial draw with Eckhard Dagge in his first world title challenge, had not tasted defeat for 6 long years. Fighting away from home was unlikely to phase a man who had previously performed in hostile environments, not least when he stopped Mattioli in his own backyard. "He had the Mafia supporting him but they couldn't help him in there, could they..?" reasoned Hope. "I had to wait until I came back to England to celebrate because they were very hostile in Italy... It was very frightening. All my supporters got 'kicked in.'" On this occasion, Maurice was planning to celebrate, win or lose, having resolved to marry his girlfriend in 'Sin City' immediately after the fight.

Benitez, who had been known to celebrate before fights let alone afterwards, maintained his eccentric habits, apparently unimpressed with the enormity of the task ahead. Days before the show, when the challenger ought to have been deep in the final throes of preparation, Jim Jacobs later revealed, "Wilfred suddenly broke training, stole off and took a 3-day vacation, to my amazement." Such foibles were part and parcel of an extraordinary package, the manager admitted. "I agree that he is unreliable sometimes but I still think he is the greatest fighter in the world." The inadvisability of his impromptu sabbatical was perhaps confirmed at the weigh in when Benitez required a stint in the sauna before tipping the scales at 153 and a quarter pounds at the second time of asking. His welterweight days were almost certainly in the rear view mirror.

A shirtless Wilfred appeared almost vacantly serene when interviewed by Gil Clancy in his dressing room ahead of the CBS Saturday afternoon broadcast. What would it mean to him to join the elite band of men who laid claim to a trilogy of world championships..? "It make me feel very great… like a boxer.. and I think this is a chance in my life to win another title and bring it back to Puerto Rico," he murmured as Goyo laced his left glove. Sugar Ray Leonard was on hand in the opposing locker room to ask the champion how he felt about walking to the ring as a 3/1 underdog. "Well, it makes me very enthusiastic," retorted Hope. "The story of my life… I've always been an underestimated fighter and I'm here to show America that I'm a good fighter than they expect. (sic)"

Not content to wait for the first bell, Benitez attempted to get under Hope's skin as soon as the champion entered the ring with a truculent display of jostling and glaring before referee, Richard Green, ushered him away. Wearing a half smile that denoted his embarrassment, Maurice remained impassive amid the preponderance of jeers greeted that his opponent's name when Chuck Hull introduced the principals. Although mathematically outnumbered in a crowd of mostly high rollers at the Caesars Sports Pavilion, Hope's vocal supporters club did their best to recreate the ambience of Wembley Arena - cheering their man with the same raucous enthusiasm with which they had booed his opponent. When the fighters came together for the obligatory pre -fight cautions, Benitez made one last attempt to ruffle his prey. "While the referee was giving us instructions, he pushed me and that riled me," confessed Hope. "I forgot about the pace and wanted to kick his face in."

For 3 rounds, Benitez hardly resembled the 'greatest fighter in the world' as he skittered around the ring, allowing the champion to plod forward in a manner that Clancy likened to 'Hopalong Cassidy', dictating behind a stiff southpaw jab. Lending credence to rumours of an injured left hand, Wilfred seemed overly reliant on right leads and was uncharacteristically crude in his delivery - often throwing arcs and loops. "I've never seen Benitez this wild, Ray, he's really winging his punches.. some of them are very, very wide," remarked Clancy to his illustrious ringside colleague. The pattern continued when Hope outworked Benitez in the fourth, opening a cut in the corner of the challenger's right eye as the London contingent chanted 'LET'S GO, SUPER MO' with vociferous monotony. The upset was looking vaguely plausible until Benitez nailed Hope with a straight right hand in the dwindling seconds of Round 5 that backed the champion to the ropes as the bell sounded. And then came the turning point.

As if the first 15 minutes had been a dress rehearsal, Benitez stepped on the gas in Round 6 and hurt Maurice with a right hand left / left hook that had him holding momentarily in the challenger's corner. Manoeuvring his quarry back into ring centre, he threaded another perfect right cross through the Englishman's guard which opened the floodgates for a savage two fisted barrage of unanswered hooks. Battered unmercifully against the ropes, it was a testament to Hope's raw grit that he remained erect for a further 30 seconds but suddenly he'd found himself in a fire fight with a pen - knife. Mindful of that equation, Maurice attempted to crowd his man in the 7th as the two went toe to toe but it was the challenger who constantly landed the more hurtful blows as Gil Clancy concluded, "He's falling into Benitez' trap now."

Hope continued to press the action for the next two rounds as Benitez was content to lure the champion onto the ropes, where he was able to counterpunch at mid-range and dominate on the inside. Midway through the ninth, Hope spat out a tooth through blood smeared lips and, in the 10th, a counter right hand reunited him with the ivory fragment that had fallen to the canvas. Saved by the bell, he resembled a man sleep walking through mud as he trudged back to the corner to absorb whatever words of wisdom his manager., Terry Lawless, could muster. Still averse to the notion of defeat, Hope landed a big overhand left in the eleventh although Benitez was visibly untroubled by its impact. The diametric opposite was true when the latter feinted a jab to the body in Round 12 before the lowering the boom with a devastating overhand right that felled Hope like a tree. The new champion's immediate reaction to the chilling sight of his stricken foe's comatose form twitching involuntarily on the deck was rather tasteless and incongruent as he threw his mouthpiece into the crowd and noisily celebrated with his acolytes.

Hope was out cold for 3 minutes, with almost 10 minutes elapsing before the attendant physicians decreed him fit to leave the ring under his own steam. From there he went to the nearby Valley Hospital and was detained overnight for precautionary checks before marrying his fiancé as planned. Nursing nicks over both eyes at a crowded press conference, Wilfred attempted to explain the dichotomy of the hurt business in his threadbare second language:

"Outside the ring he is my brother but this is business... big, big business. I hit him too much plenty hard. When I hit him the last time, I feel it through my hand."

When asked how it had felt to see Hope unconscious, he replied, "It felt good. Suppose you're in the ring - how do you feel...? Great, right..? We are boxers. Here, now, we are brothers but in the ring.... forget it..! Now I want Sugar Ray Leonard, we'll make many millions of dollars - enough to buy Puerto Rico. Then the middleweight title. Though after this, Marvin Hagler will want to step up a division."

Reacting to the news that his opponent had lost a couple of teeth along with the WBC belt, he resorted to his native Spanish: "Puedes poner tus dientes debajo de la almohada." Translation - "He can put the teeth under his pillow."

Whilst finding Benitez 'very callous', Hope's veteran promoter, Mickey Duff, had no reservations regarding his exceptional qualities inside the squared circle. "After seeing this tonight, I'm more convinced than ever that it was making the weight that beat Benitez in the Leonard fight. The guy punched too quickly for Maurice and it would be the same if he met Hagler. I'm absolutely positive he would win that one."

In the wake of an historical triumph, even Goyo was inclined to superlatives. "Tonight was my son's finest fight. Winning a world title for the first time was sweet but this was Wilfred's greatest hour. Now there are so many things we can aim for and achieve."

12/ VOODOO IN VEGAS

Taboo it may be, but history has shown that fighters are occasionally given to prognostications both dark and unsavoury in the exacting period that precedes a fight. With few exceptions, the daily pressures of training, sparring and making weight have never been known to expose the lighter side of a boxer's character. It might have been residual bad blood - or simply the thought of losing his crown to a fellow Puerto Rican - that fuelled Wilfred's vow to end Carlos Santos' life along with his title aspirations on November 14.

"I'll knock him out. I'll kill him. I'm going to make sure he goes to the cemetery," swore the new champion.

Figuratively speaking, Santos had already died a death when he appeared on the Hope - Benitez undercard and laboured to stop a Texan trial horse by the name of Raul Aguirre in 5 rounds. Although soundly beaten and floored 3 times, Aguirre - described in Boxing News as 'unbelievably crude' - buckled the favourite's knees in the first round with a Hail Mary left swing and briefly threatened to upset the apple cart. The left hook that eventually poleaxed the squat Chicano brawler was conclusive enough but in the estimation of the esteemed British journal 'it was hardly a performance to give the new world champion sleepless nights.' That said, Santos was undefeated in 22 starts and ranked No.1 by the WBC despite an absence of top tier opposition on his resume. 3 years older than Benitez, he had turned pro 3 years later after representing Puerto Rico in the 1976 Olympics at welterweight. Since 1980, the stylish if unspectacular southpaw had based himself in Italy in an effort to cultivate his rarity value in a culture less renowned for world class fighters. Confident that his Island compatriot posed little threat, Benitez had already signed to meet Roberto Duran for global Latin bragging rights on January 30.

The most remarkable thing about the first ever world title clash between two Puerto Ricans fighters was, in the main, precisely that. There were boos as early as the first round at the Showboat Casino in Las Vegas as a crowd of 3000 bore witness to a cerebral feinting contest in the vain hope that a fight would break out. At the end of Round 3, alluding to transmission problems at the beginning of the HBO broadcast, Larry Merchant quipped, "So far, I wish the video hadn't returned." Benitez was credited with a knockdown in Round 6 when he appeared to miss with a right uppercut before knocking the challenger off balance with his shoulder but he had Santos legitimately in trouble in the eleventh which proved to be the most action packed of 15 long stanzas. 3 minutes earlier, Merchant had informed the viewers that he had the contest 'dead even' but thereafter the champion's greater experience and willingness to make a fight proved the difference against a man who had never been past 8 rounds. In the final frame, Benitez wobbled his taller opponent with a short right hook but had to make do with a unanimous decision in a maiden defence that had been forgettable beyond its bare statistics. Asked by Larry Merchant if he was unhappy with his performance, oblivious to the negative prefix, Wilfred replied, "Yes, I'm happy. I don't care if the people like it but.. next time, I hope I will make it better... Against Roberto Duran, I will continue training and I know that I can beat him easy."

The Duran fight was still a big deal in the trade although the Panamanian legend's brand had lost some of its lustre due to the ignominious nature of his loss to Ray Leonard in November 1980. After recording one of the greatest wins in boxing history, Roberto had succumbed to the notorious gluttony that often marked his periods of idleness- piling on the pounds with alacrity as he partied on a permanent loop in his homeland. If his ballooning weight was not sufficient cause for concern then a plenitude of loose women and free flowing liquor served to further undermine his manhood as the hot days turned into hot nights in a frenzied blur of indulgence. Receiving word of Duran's condition on the grapevine, Leonard's team conspired to strike while the iron was hot, effectively fast tracking the rematch by virtue of an $8 million guarantee to sign on the dotted line. When Duran received a call from Don King in early September informing him of the imminent November date, some sources claimed the WBC Welterweight Champion weighed as much as 190 pounds.

Offering a more conservative estimate, co-trainer Freddie Brown said his man scaled 173 at the beginning of a chaotic training camp in upstate New York, hampered at every turn by the profusion of spurious free loaders who had attached themselves to the champ since his epic victory in the summer. Brown, a flat nosed Runyonesque character who might have been mocked up for the movies, was aghast. "In my nearly 70 years in boxing, I've never seen such a bunch of losers in my life. They had Duran convinced that he couldn't live without them. Those leaches suck all da' fight out of him. They had him talking all these diet pills and starving himself." By the first week of November, Roberto was still a middleweight and 3 days before the fight (on November 22) he weighed

157 lbs - 10 pounds north of the championship ceiling. With drastic measures required, Carlos Eleta claimed that Duran used a diuretic to help him shed the excess bulk although the fighter himself and his personal physician, Dr. Orlando Nunez, refuted the manager's version of events. What is documented is that Duran came in a pound under the limit at the official midday weigh in, held on the day of the fight at the Hyatt Regency Hotel in New Orleans. But it was alleged by various credible sources that the severely dehydrated former lightweight king hadn't eaten for 60 hours before he stepped on the scales.

In the company of guest photographer and supermodel, Christie Brinkley, Ring Magazine's Randy Gordon watched in wonder as Duran - his contractual obligation fulfilled - immediately devoured two huge grapefruits and a cup of hot broth before heading to the atrium dining area with single minded haste. Thereafter, by Gordon's account, the fighter wolfed down a pair of 16oz steaks with two steaming baked potatoes plus a large salad and a surfeit of waffles, pancakes and French toast - his digestion 'aided' by gallons of grapefruit juice and hot tea. According to Freddie Brown and head coach, Ray Arcel, Duran then retired to his room for a nap before waking up at around 4.30 pm with a fresh appetite. Attempting to make peace with his body for the 2 and half day fast, Duran ordered another large steak and another baked potato with yet more fruit juice to wash it down. Even without the benefit of 'modern nutrition', it was as plain an example of madness as could be found in a subculture that boasted an entry level of dysfunction.

The fight itself bore no resemblance to its classic predecessor as Leonard made full use of his superior hand and foot speed versus a sluggish impersonator of the man who had snapped his unbeaten record. For 6 rounds Duran struggled to find his floating adversary and, when he did, he invariably got the worst of the argument, the challenger repeatedly nailing him with crisp, spiteful combinations off a rapier left jab. In the 7th round, Leonard showboated outrageously, dropping his hands and shimmying as he dared the champion to take a shot at his protruding jaw. Sensing that the man in front of him was a depleted force, the Sugarman broke into an Ali shuffle before windmilling his right hand theatrically only to spear Duran with a jarring straight left. It was juvenile, unbecoming and beautiful all at once.

Roberto's reaction to such an unthinkable humiliation was delayed by approximately 4 minutes when he suddenly turned and quit at 2.44 of Round 8, allegedly uttering the now infamous words, 'NO MAS.' Although Duran later claimed to have said something more expansively critical of his flashy opponent, it afforded him no dispensation from the rancour incurred by his abject surrender. Officially, the withdrawal was blamed on chronic stomach cramps but most observers surmised that the pathologically proud Latino was simply unwilling to take a beating - particularly if it came with a side order of ridicule. The backslash was resounding and vitriolic, especially in Panama where Duran had previously enjoyed God like status. Subsequently, a brace of rehabilitative wins over Nino Gonzalez and Luigi Minchillo had done nothing to erase the stigma.

If the National affection for Duran had curdled then the Panamanian Government hadn't entirely given up on its fallen idol. For Benitez, he had planned to train in Los Angeles but, fearing that 'Tinsel Town' represented an all

108

too familiar playground, Eleta and the ill fated General Omar Torrijos conspired to sequester their man on the Island of Coiba, a penal colony 15 miles off the coast of Panama. There were no cells containing the 350 odd 'inmates' but the shark infested waters that surrounded the island tended to serve as a deterrent for would be escapers. Mingling with some of Panama's most dangerous criminals, the former street urchin is said to have felt right at home. "It turned out to be a master stroke," admitted his close adviser, Luis Henriquez. "All the prisoners know what hard times are and it didn't bother them what Roberto had done in New Orleans. They did wonders building his morale. And with no distractions, he became hard and mean once more."

Quite how hard Benitez had worked in the same time frame was open to conjecture. Speaking days before the fight in his Las Vegas hotel suite, Wilfred told an interviewer, "I have trained right. I lost the weight by training instead of just not eating - but this weight is too hard to make anymore. But I feel strong because I have worked very hard. At this weight, I and not Duran will have the hands of stone." Reiterating his desire to conquer new worlds, he promised, "This is my last fight as a junior middleweight and it is very important. After this fight, I want to become a middleweight and beat Marvin Hagler for my fourth title. For this I must be disciplined."

When asked about the discipline his son had shown in camp, Goyo snapped, "I got nothing to say about that." Immediately contradicting himself, he continued. "I think he could have trained better this time. This is going to be a furious fight. This is a fight for Latin America and the Americans are all eager to see my champion beat Duran.

We have to beat him any way we can. Kicking if we have to…. Duran's a dirty fighter. Everybody knows he is a street fighter…. all of Wilfred's fights have been clean."

Wilfred had been known to go missing before but several weeks earlier whilst still in Puerto Rico, Goyo had received a telephone call from a party unknown who claimed to have kidnapped the WBC junior-middleweight champion and duly demanded a million dollars for his safe return. "Kill him," Goyo is reported to have said before hanging up abruptly. In view of a parental ethos that fell well shy of mollycoddling, one can only hope he took it to be a hoax. Something he took more seriously was a warning that the Panamanians intended to use voodoo against him on the premise that Gregorio Sr was a 'witch.' According to Pat Putnam writing for Sports Illustrated, the old man posted guards in vigil and constantly searched the suite for 'suspicious powders' or marks on the doors. It was better to be safe than sorry.

At the final press conference, Goyo told Duran scathingly, "We have trained to fight 15 rounds, just in case you decide not to quit in the eighth round." Taking the barb in good humour, Duran laughed and informed the assembled media: "After I beat Wilfred I am going to get Don King to sign my father to fight his father." Regarding the remark as incendiary, Wilfred jumped out of his seat and attempted to get at Roberto who laughed some more. "All of Benitez' clowning just proves he's afraid of me. I sleep nights. I am sure he doesn't."

Although their rivalry had been simmering for half a dozen years, Duran effectively saw Benitez as a stepping stone to the revenge he craved. "I'm fighting Benitez to

get one more chance at Ray Leonard," he conceded.
"Leonard is my ultimate goal." 9 months before his shock
retirement, Leonard agreed that he was living in both
fighters' heads rent free.

"They'll be throwing punches at each other but they'll
really be aiming at me. They know where the 'pot' is. I'll
probably accommodate the winner."

13/ CROWNING GLORY

"I don't want a fencing match," insisted Ray Arcel. "That's his game. We got to fight him for 15 rounds." It was noteworthy that Arcel had a professional opinion to offer, having initially sworn to cease working with Duran after the shame of 'No Mas.' Temporarily true to his word, Ray had sat out the Gonzalez and Minchillo affairs before Carlos Eleta convinced the octogenarian sage to give his fighter another chance. "Who knows what happened that night..?" the old man reflected. "Not even Duran can explain it. Can you condemn a man for one mistake..? When Eleta called me, I told him if Duran was ever in a big fight I would be there." Effectively precluding any excuses for a subpar performance, Arcel echoed the testimony of Luis Henriquez. "He's been working out next to a prison in Panama and there has been no nonsense. He is the best conditioned Roberto Duran I ever saw."

If redemption meant more to Duran than the half million-dollar purse then Benitez' aspirations were similarly high minded said Jim Jacobs. "It's not so much the title that is motivating Wilfred. He knows about Duran as a legend and now Wilfred wants the glory and the recognition as the greatest Latin fighter." For those who measure greatness in statistics, they had but 3 losses between them from a hundred and twenty-one professional contests, each having debuted before shaving became a necessary daily ritual. The man who had dealt 2 of those losses favoured the champion "But only if he doesn't fight Duran the way I fought him in Montreal" stressed Sugar Ray Leonard, providing colour commentary for Home Box Office. The bookies agreed with him, although the starting price of 3/1 on Duran had fallen to 8/5 by the time he entered the ring at 10pm on a mild Saturday night in Vegas.

Soon, that ring was as densely populated as Grand Central Station during rush hour, with both sizeable entourages facing off like opposing factions at a protest rally, brandishing their sovereign banners and attempting to acquire importance via osmosis. At variance with standard procedure, the champion was announced first to a clamorous 4, 500 crowd that was audibly in favour of the Panamanian, diminished standing or not. Duran, resplendent in an indigo velvet robe, was apparently still the undisputed champion of Latin American fistiana and reports of his demise had been exaggerated. Benitez and his throng wore yellow, perhaps with subliminal reference to the lack of heroism Roberto had exhibited against Leonard, although it would be unwise to overthink such things.

If Duran had planned to replicate the suffocating aggression he had employed in the first Leonard fight then it wasn't evident in the opening round as both fighters took a look at each other. "He looks a little sluggish and I'm really surprised that he didn't really come in and go hard at Benitez. He's moving around and that's Benitez' fight," remarked Carlos Palomino, also working for HBO. "I think he's a little weak and that's the reason I think he's going to be sluggish throughout the fight," added Sugar Ray as the second round commenced. It was a round that saw Duran apply more pressure while Benitez fell into his familiar rope assisted escapology but the firepower associated with the fabled 'Hands of Stone' was noticeably absent. Benitez' greater hand speed and counter punching accuracy were the dominant factors in Round 3 as he repeatedly nailed Duran with lead rights

113

and lefts hooks to head and body. "There's nothing behind Duran's punches," lamented Leonard. Seeking to make a liar of his nemesis, Roberto slightly wobbled the champion with a right hand at the end of the fourth but "..otherwise Benitez was in total control of that round," thought Larry Merchant.

Duran missed more wildly than great fighters are supposed to in the fifth as Benitez continued to find a home for his surgical straight right, juxtaposed with a fluid body attack. "Don't let this bum lick you," begged Ray Arcel during the interval, perhaps thinking better of the rekindled alliance. The desperate plea seemed to fall on deaf ears until the challenger landed another big right hand in the closing seconds of Round 6 that might have rocked Benitez, though not nearly as much as an excitable Barry Tomkins encouraged the television audience to believe. Apparently bolstered by marginal success, Duran picked up the pace in Round 7, resulting in a lively even session before a Benitez right uppercut opened a cut above his left eye. "(Benitez) is probably fighting the fight of his life here and Duran - perhaps as far back as he's gone - would still beat a lot of fighters right now," observed Larry Merchant as the crowd booed at the end of a quiet 8th round.

Wilfred coasted in the ninth, bouncing vibrantly on his toes as if moving a novice around in the gym before 'sitting down' on his punches in the next frame and appearing to hurt Duran several times with right hands and left hooks. Although Arcel had pledged that his man would 'kill himself first' before quitting again, there remained an air of resignation about Duran's plodding efforts in the 11th as Benitez continued to have things his own way. 'Investing in the body' the champion repeatedly made unauthorised withdrawals from his opponent's reserves of vitality, with energy sapping shots downstairs. "Right now on my card, Duran needs a knockout and there might not be a harder man in the world to knock out than Benitez," speculated Merchant ahead of Round 12.

As fate decreed, Duran would have to make do with drawing blood in the twelfth - from a cut over Wilfred's left eye - and landing another potent right hand before being outworked once again in the thirteenth. Although one of the ringside arbiters turned out to have the fight implausibly close, it was hard to pinpoint a single stanza in which Duran had been undeniably superior. At 30 years of age, in his 77th prize fight, he was apparently approaching athletic senility in an era when performance enhancing drugs, inactivity and cautious matchmaking had yet to extend the primes of world class fighters to the brink of their 40s. What price that he would yet outlive his adversary in the fight game's upper echelon..? Nostradamus would likely have hedged his bets.

Imperiously immune to fatigue in spite of his training habits, Benitez cruised the fourteenth round, dictating from mid-range and flurrying whenever Duran got too close. With reference to the champion's unassailable lead, Merchant informed his colleagues: "I've given him (Duran) 2 rounds so far." Groping for small mercies, Tompkins interjected, "He has not embarrassed himself tonight." The narrative of the legend's partial redemption outweighing the brilliance of the man who was giving him a boxing lesson was inescapable.

"This may be the last round you will ever see Roberto Duran fight," warned Merchant as the bell chimed for

Round 15 and the still optimistic Panamanian contingent chanted their familiar refrain. ('DOO - RAN... DOO - RAN...!') Although Roberto had occasionally borne the sobriquet, this was no 'Rocky' movie and the raucous din did nothing to extricate him from the tiredness and lethargy incurred in the course of a thoroughly frustrating evening. Seeking to underline his casual dominance, Benitez spent the last 60 seconds of the fight with his back to a neutral corner, outfoxing and out - punching the challenger with ludicrous ease. At the bell, his magnanimous attempt to embrace Duran was spurned with a truculent hand gesture from the master of sour grapes, who walked away in disgust. Amused by the lack of sportsmanship, Wilfred wound up his right hand a la Sugar Ray Leonard and followed Duran around the ring until the latter's handlers intervened.

As the ring filled up once more with extraneous bodies, both fighters were hoisted aloft but only Team Puerto Rico looked authentic in its exultation. If Dave Moretti's 144 - 141 card seemed a tad generous to Duran then Hal Miller's single point margin for Benitez was a bad joke. Only in boxing can judges, either incompetent or bent, hide behind their divine right to 'subjectivity' but at least he had rendered the third score academic and found the right winner. Lou Tabat was closest to transcribing what Carlos Palomino saw as 'a lopsided win for Benitez' with a total of 145 - 141, the announcement of which cued predictable celebrations from the Benitez clan - the young champion flexing his biceps with that distinctive adolescent charm.

"I needed a little more training," Duran told Larry Merchant in the immediate aftermath. When asked if TOO MUCH training might have been the issue, it was clear that Roberto's psyche was comfortable with either explanation as he shrugged, "Could be..." Benitez, in his estimation, was, "Very good...good boxer but he ran a lot from me...."

"I was too strong," countered Wilfred after making some opaque allusions to his market value and asking price for a Ray Leonard rematch. "I have a radar in my eyes... nobody in boxing have my style. I'm the king of style...." With respect to his future plans, the WBC junior middleweight titlist appeared to say that he was "...all ready for Marvin Hagler on June the 29th...." his still threadbare English impeding full comprehension.

An hour or so later, at a crowded post fight presser in a small interview room at the Caesars Palace Sports Pavilion, Wilfred gave generous to a man he described as one of his boyhood idols. Duran - seated next to him - was 'the champion of contenders' and the glory of his victory belonged to Latin American boxing and "all the Puerto Ricans."

"How good is Marvin Hagler," asked one scribe after promoter, Don King, offered the undisputed middleweight champ a cool 3 million dollars to face Benitez in the summer. "I think he is marvelous," replied Wilfred, consciously citing Marvin's legal nom de guerre. Explaining his charge's willingness to address the media in English - unlike Duran who had never made such a concession - Jim Jacobs admitted, "We felt he should make a concerted attempt to speak English. He was unintentionally alienating a lot of people by not conversing in English. But when he tries to express himself in English, so many thoughts are misunderstood and misrepresented. When he's showcased in the ring...

every nuance is interpreted but it's a calculated risk permitting him to communicate in English when he's infinitely more superior in another language."

Whilst the pressmen and even his own manager attempted to banish Duran into premature retirement, high hopes abounded for the continued rise of his conqueror, now thought to be in possession of the emotional maturity to match his boundless talent. "There's been a dramatic philosophical change in Wilfred in the last year and a half," claimed Jacobs. "What we saw against Duran was another example of this change."

2 days later in the New York Times, Neil Amdur proclaimed, 'The Roberto Duran saga has ended, but the greening of Wilfred Benitez may be just beginning.'

The article hasn't aged well but few would have disagreed at the time.

14/ THE HITMAN AND HER

If Duran and Benitez had been deeply impacted by their respective losses to Sugar Ray Leonard then Tommy Hearns had taken his harder still, on all available evidence. On September 16, 1981, the 'Hitman' had turned 'Hit and Run Man' in the richest fight in boxing history, coming within 4 minutes and 15 seconds of a sensational triumph before yielding to a desperate rally that might conceivably have vanquished King Kong. Thereafter, according to his intimates, the deposed WBA welterweight king went into self imposed isolation for 72 hours to lick his psychological wounds. Part of Hearns' emotional indigestion was rooted in denial as he insisted that Davey Pearl's 14th round intervention had been premature and that he could have continued. Feeling that his victory was unfairly besmirched by such a contention, Leonard refused to entertain the notion of a rematch until Hearns conceded his superiority. "Tommy won't retract the statement because he honestly believes he could have gone on," explained Hearns' mentor and Kronk Gym supremo, Manny Steward. "It's not unusual. Here was a boxer who had never been stopped before. He doesn't know what it means to say he can't go on."

After suffering his first loss in 33 paid fights, Tommy had experienced a tougher time than expected en route to outpointing Ernie Singletary in a 10 rounder at middleweight before icing the ordinarily durable Marcos Geraldo inside a round. A massive, gangling welterweight at 6' 1", Hearns had surprised all and sundry when he came in 2 pounds under the championship limit for his unification clash with Leonard but looked infinitely more comfortable at 153 and a quarter - his given weight vs Geraldo. He had not listened and overtrained for Leonard said Steward but the bountiful diet of steak and milkshakes in the run up to his most recent blowout had met with the fighter's approval. "Training has been real nice this time," he acknowledged. A few more steaks down the line, Hearns had planned to challenge for Marvin Hagler's undisputed middleweight crown in another gate busting extravaganza on May 24 (and latterly July 15) before talks between the two sides suddenly collapsed. Bob Arum blamed the fight's demise on increased financial demands from the Hearns camp whilst Hagler preferred to believe that Tommy was simply afraid of him. Steward, for his part, charged Arum - a legendary exponent of double-talk - with failing to keep his word. After the original date fell through, the promoter reportedly told Steward that he 'could not live up to that contract anymore' because he had lost a lawsuit to HBO, who claimed to have bought the rights.

"We were still willing to be offered a new contact," explained Steward, "but Arum offered Thomas only $500,000. Tommy said he wasn't willing to fight for that kind of money. And then Arum said if the fight were held at the Silverdome (in Pontiac, Michigan) would that entice him to take the smaller purse..? We said 'Yes' because we could draw more people there. So we made a verbal agreement on the phone for $500,000 on the gamble that Thomas would get the live gate money and that would make up for the smaller purse."

The compromise was rendered academic when Hagler refused to fight in his opponent's home state and so Hearns and Steward turned their attention to Benitez and his WBC light middleweight strap. Big fights between elite fighters were considerably easier to make in the early 1980s when the money was big but not so precariously astronomical as to create insurmountable stumbling blocks. Accordingly, on June 18, 1982, Steward informed United Press International that Hearns - Benitez was a done deal in principle and would likely take place in October in Las Vegas. "This is the fight we've had in the background all the time," he explained. "We could have taken it any time we wanted but Thomas purposely wanted to get Hagler for personal reasons. He felt it would give him more credibility." Optimistically, the manager/ trainer reckoned both fighters would earn around three million dollars apiece.

Benitez, who had earned roughly half that amount vs Duran, had been inactive in the time that had since elapsed. In a Ring magazine cover story entitled 'WHAT'S NEXT FOR THE TRIPLE CROWN CHAMP?', compatriot and former light heavyweight king, Jose Torres, wrote on the gulf that existed between the 23-year old's ring savvy and his personal development:

'He anticipates punches as if he had a highly sophisticated radar hidden somewhere in his soul. He moves and punches with the confidence of a seasoned master, incapable of making one single mistake. His performances are overwhelming. But then you get him outside the ring and his nothingness underwhelms you. It becomes quite difficult for him to form an intelligent conversation.'

Benitez, suggested Torres, was a fighter who had matured 'but only pugilistically ; that his life outside the ring reflected the conduct and behaviour of a child.' In the same article, Goyo - having ousted Emile Griffith from his auxiliary coaching role several fights ago - turned his attention to Jim Jacobs. "Once our contract with Jacobs runs out.... we are going to get rid of him. We won't need him anymore. We really didn't need him to be where we are." Not buying into the notion of a dubiously qualified control freak, Jose described Gregorio Sr as 'a very good trainer' and 'a positive force in his son's career.'

With negotiations ongoing, Hearns took a tune up fight on July 25 against undefeated middleweight, Jeff McCracken at the Cobo Hall in his native Detroit. McCracken, who had questioned Tommy's power at 160, was dropped twice in the second round before being stopped in the eighth whilst on the receiving end of a vicious, all inclusive battery against the ropes. Talking to Tim Ryan during the post-fight interview, the winner revealed, "I think I'm gonna' take another tune up fight and after this next tune up fight, maybe I'll go for it...I'll go for the championship next. I hope it'll be Benitez and I'm looking forward to a fight with Benitez."

Despite his previously avowed intentions to the contrary, Wilfred proved willing to subject himself to the rigours of making 154 lbs again for an initial guarantee of $1.5 million dollars. Hearns, the naturally bigger man who had scaled 159 and 3 quarters for McCracken, apparently didn't struggle to sweat his triangular frame down to light middleweight and would receive purse parity. At a press conference on November 16, promoter Don King announced that the winner of the December 3 fight at the New Orleans Superdome would be rewarded with a shot at Marvin Hagler in 'the first quarter of 1983.' A week earlier, Sugar Ray Leonard had sensationally announced his retirement at a gala ceremony in Baltimore following corrective surgery to repair a detached retina. Hagler had been present and correct, labouring under the misapprehension that Leonard had assembled the world's media to announce a super fight between the two. Realising that he had been hoodwinked, the 'Marvelous One' is said to have never gotten over the resentment.

Faithful to the old axiom about the best laid schemes of mice and men, King's financial calculations began to go awry in the days leading up to the fight. Initially, the 'Only In America' man had hoped to attract 40,000 fans to the Superdome plus 40 percent of a potential 2 and a half million pay per view audience. Suddenly fearing that the actual attendance would amount to less than half of the original projection, King asked both teams to accept a pay cut of $250,000. 2 days before the bout, Steward detailed his fighter's frustration to Pete Alfano of the New York Times:

"About a week ago, Don King asked us to take a substantial cut. I'm not going to say what it was but it is substantial. And that's why Thomas is upset. He has made every effort to promote the fight. He broke training last week to go to the Holmes - Cobb fight; he rode in that (Mardi Gras) parade here on Monday when he could have been getting a rubdown. He was the only fighter in the parade and he feels his image has been damaged."

Hearns and Steward accepted the reduced purse because Benitez agreed to forfeit the same sum after Jim Jacobs proposed that both fighters take a 'haircut' in order to save the fight. Wilfredo Gomez and Lupe Pintor, who would make up the co - feature on a show billed as 'The Carnival Of Champions', were each obliged to take a $125,000 hit on their previous 'guarantees' of $750,000. Steward was inclined to take a philosophical view of the situation. "Boxing is reeling already," he said in allusion to the tragic Ray Mancini - Deuk Koo Kim fight 3 weeks earlier. "What good would it do to walk out and have a cancellation..? But Thomas has made up his mind that he has done all he can and that he is through with publicity."

Unlike his opponent, the champion felt no obligation to promote the fight and was merely concerned with the serious business of training, he insisted. Observing that Wilfred appeared to be sparring inordinately hard a few days before the fight, a journalist asked about the rumours he had only been working in earnest for 3 weeks. "This happens all the time," scoffed Benitez. "I'm in great shape. People say this because they don't want to see me win. I'm too good, though, and in this fight, I will show my ability. After this fight, I will be recognised." Echoing the tasteless ambience of his comments before the sleep inducing Santos affair, he boasted, "I will kill Hearns. Yes, I will kill him."

Manny Steward remained unconvinced of his star fighter's impending mortality. "Benitez is not the puncher that Leonard was. He doesn't have a single punch that can turn a fight around. But he is a great boxer and he has great stamina. And his place in boxing is written in stone."

If Wilfred's legacy was etched in such solidity then it was stone that the fighters appeared hell bent on converting one another into during a pre-fight stare down that rivalled the Leonard - Benitez face off for its intensity. The latter, once described in print as 'a strutting macho kid, not playing with a full deck', echoed those words when he shoved the challenger but there was no retaliation as Hearns maintained his iconically baleful glare for another 20 seconds. Benitez, clad in black velvet trunks with a white trim, was decidedly less confrontational when the bell rang, moving side to side and feinting at a stalking nemesis who resembled a skinny light heavyweight in comparison. Nominating himself as the subliminal 'good guy', Hearns wore white satin and landed the first scoring blow with a rapid straight right to the body after 2 minutes of mutual posturing. "Benitez didn't land a single punch," said Larry Merchant as the round came to a close. "I think that was a very good round for Tommy Hearns because he went to the body - you can't headhunt with Benitez, he's just too quick."

Benitez kept his distance in the second as if wary of mounting an offensive against a wrecking ball puncher with 78 inches of fast twitch leverage. Although he won the round by virtue of his opponent's pacifism, Hearns' frustration was evident in the last 30 seconds when he continually swatted thin air as Benitez dipped and swayed in his own corner, like a low flying kite in a violent gale. "Benitez hardly landed anything worthwhile in that round again and we may see a fighter being intimidated," though Merchant from the safety of ringside. The next two rounds followed much the same the pattern until referee, Octavio Meyran, bizarrely deducted a point from Hearns at the end of the fourth for pushing the champion's head down with his left forearm. "That being the case, that was Benitez' best round..!" quipped Merchant, seemingly never short of satire.

Hearns claimed the stolen point back in the fifth when he scored the quintessence of a flash knockdown with a chopping right hand that caused Wilfred to touch down with both gloves before springing back up on rickety legs. Meyran's mandatory 8 count was met with a truculent shrug but this time the third man had gotten it right. "He has to fight Tommy," concluded Ray Leonard midway through Round 6. "He can't just stand back because Tommy's arms are so long, so Benitez has to 'street fight' him." As if he might have heard his former conqueror, Wilfred span Hearns into a neutral corner and attempted open up on the challenger's midsection but soon found himself tied up and driven to an adjacent corner, under heavy fire. Suddenly, the 'radar' was proving only 50 percent effective in neutralising the constant flow of leather from arguably the finest offensive fighter in the world. 5 seconds before the bell, Benitez knees buckled alarmingly from the same straight right hand that had turned Pipino Cuevas into a noodle, prompting the Sugarman to observe. "Benitez just stumbled back to his corner, he's really hurt."

After an even seventh round, Hearns went on his bike in the eighth as Benitez made a concerted effort to press the action for the first time. Any judge who favoured aggression for its own sake, might conceivably have given both rounds to the champion. Wilfred received a further boost in Round 9 when he was awarded a spurious knockdown after landing a glancing left jab to the top of his opponent's Afro. "I no hit him," he would later admit. "But as he started to fall, I think he try to kick me so I step on his foot." Aside from the referee's bad call, the key takeaway was that Hearns appeared to have stopped throwing his vaunted right hand, perhaps due to an injury incurred in the previous round. "He never told me until after the fight," said Steward with reference to the moment when Hearns caught Benitez high on the head and immediately felt something 'give.' "He said he knew I was already too nervous and he didn't want to make it worse for me. I couldn't understand it. He was setting up

Benitez beautifully for the right hand and then he never threw it."

When he wasn't rendering opponents horizontal, Hearns had an alternative moniker that harked back to the amateurs jabber he had been before the onset of man strength had made him an assassin. And so, with the 'Hitman' unavailable, he reverted to the 'Motor City Cobra', moving, jabbing and left hooking in the tenth like a man on a unicycle armed with a cattle prod. Embracing Plan B, Tommy won rounds 11 and 12 at a canter as Benitez alternated between playing possum on the ropes and attempting to close the distance. Bearing testimony to the challenger's superiority, he was bleeding from the nose and sported a mouse over his right eye. Sorely in want of a crucial sound byte - in the manner of Angelo Dundee's legendary exhortation to Sugar Ray Leonard in the same scenario (YOU'RE BLOWING IT SON!) - an air of despondency reigned in the Benitez corner. "This is the 13th and Wilfred Benitez is simply running out of time," announced Barry Tomkins with reference to the gravity of his predicament.

Aided by the challenger's fistic impairment, Benitez advanced with impunity in the 13th and 14th rounds albeit with scant success in the grand scheme of a dialogue in which he had struggled to assert himself from the opening bell. He might at least have shaded the final session but the glee with which Wilfred embraced his foe at the bout's conclusion surely owed more to relief than any sense of premature vindication. Apparently subscribing to the early 20th century theory which stated that a champion who remained erect could not forfeit his laurels, Lou Fillipo scored the fight a draw at 142 apiece. Fortunately, the Californian's absurd Interpretation was overruled by Tony Castellano and Dick Young who saw it for the new champion by respective margins of 144-139 and 146-137.[6]

With his arm around the victor, Wilfred was supremely gracious during the HBO 'postmortem' although his father was rather less magnanimous. "The judges are a bunch of crooks," spat Goyo in the dressing room. "For the last 7 or 8 rounds the other guy was on a bicycle with his right hand stuck up his behind and they take the title away from a 3-time world champion." Quizzed about the possibility of a rematch, he shot back, "Who needs it..? One robbery is enough. One thing Hearns does is run and if a boxer who runs can beat a triple champion, who needs him..? I saw Cassius Clay run and they give to him. Maybe everybody just wants to destroy boxing. We fight Marvin Hagler. If not him then I tell Wilfred to retire."

Weeks after losing his crown, in January 1983, Wilfred married Elizabeth Alonso - his 'childhood sweetheart' who lived across the street from the Benitez family home in Carolina. It was a union that drove a wedge between father and son and divided the family in a way that never truly healed according to Wilfred's mother, Clara. With Goyo disapproving of the relationship for whatever reason, the newly weds moved to New York City where Wilfred began working with Victor Machado and Cus D'Amato with a view to resuming his career at middleweight. "You are married and you are a big man now. You know how to walk in New York City," Goyo said simply. Despite the mystique that surrounded D'Amato,

---

[6] On the night, Young's score was announced by Jimmy Lennon Snr as 146-136

Benitez claimed that where was nothing either he or Machado could teach him about the sweet science:

"My father showed me how to take care of myself when I am not with him. But my father is taking care of business in Puerto Rico. He's doing good. Someday he'll be in my corner again. Never should a son give his back to his father. I trust my father. I believe in him."

15/ THE ROAD TO NOWHERE

Perhaps feeling the need to reinvent himself as a threat to the world's leading middleweights, Wilfred cut a resplendent figure as he walked to the ring on a sunny afternoon in Las Vegas on May 18, 1983. Swathed in a burgundy tuxedo pastiche in lieu of the traditional robe, he was admittedly a tad overdressed for Tony Cerda, an unremarkable club fighter from California with a record of 16-2-4. His sartorial efforts notwithstanding, there were copious empty seats in the outdoor arena chiefly assembled for Bruce Curry's bid to relieve 'Irish' Leroy Haley of the WBC light welterweight strap at the Dunes Hotel and Country Club. Made to work for it by an opponent who had nothing to lose, Benitez turned in a workmanlike performance, taking a unanimous decision over 10 torridly competitive rounds. Aesthetically, he carried the extra poundage well but his inability to put a dent in Cerda throughout 30 minutes of toe-to-toe combat was unlikely to have given Marvin Hagler any sleepless nights. Covering the action for Sports Illustrated, Pat Putnam described Benitez' performance as 'dismal.'

Not sufficiently discouraged by his initial bloody battering at the hands of Marvelous Marvin, Mustafa Hamsho wanted a rematch. Being as Hamsho - a face first, marauding southpaw from Brooklyn by way of Syria - was the WBC's No. 1 contender, it was a fight that made sense to Jim Jacobs as he plotted the next move. "What have we got to lose..?" he reasoned. "If Wilfred beats Hamsho, then we fight for the middleweight title. If we lose, we'll still be the mandatory challenger to Hearns for the junior middleweight championship." The 12-round eliminator was made for July 16 at the Dunes on a Don

King promotion optimistically billed as 'July Fist Explosion.' According to the old guru, D'Amato, Wilfred's fists were more explosive than boxing people gave him credit for:

"Now Benitez can punch a lot harder than people think. But he doesn't punch. He just comes out to outbox his opponents with his smarts. I talked to him about moving side to side and punching. With Hamsho coming on a straight line, Benitez can move to the side and hit with maximum power and not be afraid of being hit because Hamsho won't be in a position to hit him." Al Certo, who had taken over managerial duties since the death of Hamsho's beloved mentor, Paddy Flood, a few months earlier was scathingly dismissive of the triple champ's pedigree. "They're giving us a quarter million for fighting a bum, a myth," he told his new charge. "You can forget about those 3 titles, about him being a superstar. That's all media hype. He's fought only two good fighters, Sugar Ray Leonard and Hearns, and he lost to both. He beat Carlos Palomino but I think Palomino took the day off. It's going to be a piece of cake."

If such slander was merely motivational psychology then Hamsho had not been inclined to underestimate an opponent since that humbling experience nearly 2 years earlier. "I've got no excuses for the Hagler fight," he admitted. "I was too cocky. I didn't respect the guy. I wasn't worried about his punching. I didn't listen to anybody. I caught every punch he threw. Now I listen to people. I'm not fighting Benitez to get another fight at Hagler. I'm fighting for me and for Paddy. I'm fighting because I want to prove I'm No. 1..." He would receive a hundred thousand dollars more than Benitez in exchange for putting that No.1 ranking on the line and there were

132

even ludicrous noises about the winner being promoted to WBC Champion if Hagler failed to embrace the organisation's new 12 round distance in the wake of the Mancini - Kim tragedy. Had it happened, it would have been a tragedy all of its own.

The stakes were high and so was the 101-degree temperature outdoors when both fighters entered the ring at around 2.30pm on a Saturday afternoon. Hamsho, advised by cut man Al Silvani to hit his man "anywhere between his collarbones and his belt buckle," applied heavy pressure from the off, immediately seeking to assert his natural size advantage. Ordinarily comfortable laying on the ropes, Benitez looked decidedly ill at ease under a barrage of body shots, forearms and shoulders in the opening 3 minutes. When the second round commenced and the mauling continued, it soon became apparent that Wilfred's best shots were bouncing off Hamsho with no noticeable effect. The reverse was true when a piercing straight left shot through the Benitez guard and placed him on 'queer street' just as the bell sounded. Stumbling back to his corner in disarray, he was duly revived by an ammonia capsule placed furtively under his nostrils by Victor Machado who, unfortunately, was rather less furtive in his manner of disposal. It was an illicit but common practice amongst members of the old school fraternity but Victor made the mistake of dropping the empty capsule in the lap of a ringside inspector. Aware that he faced a potential thousand dollar fine, he later explained, "Everybody does it. I just got caught.... Wilfred took a heavy blow in the second round and I used it. Otherwise, in the third they would have been counting 10 over him. I'm never going to see anyone count 10 on Wilfred."

Whilst Machado's commitment to his duty of care was touching, a swift conclusive ending might ultimately have been kinder than the 12-round pummelling Benitez endured. In the third, he was battered from pillar to post and shoved to the canvas on 4 separate occasions. Although no official knockdowns were recorded, the pre-fight favourite shipped heavy leather as he staggered around the ring like a drunken man on a bouncy castle. Exhibiting remarkable recuperative powers, Benitez marginally rebounded in Round 4 but only based on the chronically low expectations he had established in the previous nine minutes. Seemingly denuded of the reflexes that had informed his uncanny defensive aptitude, he was reduced to brawling with the brawler whilst pinned in his own corner as if some undiagnosed agoraphobic condition prevented his escape.

Rounds 5 through 8 were indistinguishable from one another, save for the drama of referee, Davey Pearl, hitting the deck as the 'Syrian Buzzsaw' took a rare backward step and collided with the third man. Doggedly resistant but betraying no genuine desire to win the fight, Benitez spent the last 4 rounds in the familiar confines of the same blue corner in which he had languished all afternoon. Had the top brass at ABC realised he intended to conduct the contest in such a restricted area then they might have cut production costs in half. The scores of 118-109, 118-111 and 117-111 seemed overly generous to Benitez who had not won 20 seconds of the fight by any reasonable yardstick. Sports Illustrated scored 120 to 107 for Hamsho who broke down in tears for his late Svengali when interviewed on the ring apron immediately afterwards.
Attempting to put a positive spin on the situation, Jim Jacobs concluded, "You keep moving up until finally you

reach a plateau where the people are stronger and tougher. Hamsho was much stronger than Wilfred. I think this fight will dictate that Wilfred will fight as a junior middleweight."

The next time Wilfred stepped into the ring, 7 months later on the undercard of Thomas Hearns' first defence of his WBC light middleweight title vs Luigi Minchillo, it was without the stewardship of Jacobs who had sold the fighter his contract back. Reportedly, Benitez looked 'heavy legged' in winning a 10-round decision over Stacy McSwain, a journeyman from South Carolina who would be stopped by Britain's Errol Christie in London several weeks afterwards. With a new born baby daughter to support and the six figure purse offers dwindling, Wilfred reunited with his father as the two embarked on a crossroads fight with former WBA light middleweight champion, Davey Moore, in Monaco on July 14, 1984. If Wilfred's rise had been seen as meteoric then Moore had become a world champion in only his 9th professional outing, making 3 defences before being savaged by a rejuvenated Roberto Duran in June 1983. Like Benitez, he had rebounded with a win over an 'also ran' before rolling the dice in a battle of former champions who were both regarded as damaged goods. During ABC's prefight interview, Davey explained his raison d'etre:

"My whole career has been difficult. I've only had what...15 fights..? And I won the championship in my 9th fight, so all my fights have been difficult fights. I mean they supposed to have been difficult but I made 'em easy. So I'll make this one easy."

Positive mental attitude aside, it's unlikely that the 25-year-old native of the South Bronx anticipated just how easy it would be. It happened on a balmy night at the Stade Louis II with royalty in attendance amongst an exclusive crowd of 3000 well-heeled spectators. Throughout the formal pomp and ceremony, including 3 national anthems, Benitez fixed a steely glare on his opponent who performed a merry jig by way of contrast. When the bell rang, the fighters - wearing nearly identical cerise trunks - spent 90 seconds circling one another and looking for openings before Moore suddenly found one. Felled like a ton of bricks by a basic double jab/ right hand combo, Benitez looked alarmingly vulnerable when he arose shaking his head like a wet dog emerging from the sea and kicking out his legs in an effort to recover his balance. The radar, though, had not entirely deserted him and when Moore moved in the for the 'kill' he was made to miss with several more punches than he landed in the Benitez corner as a shot fighter summoned the last remnants of his magic. Avoiding the ignominy of a first round KO defeat, Wilfred sat on his stool and received an urgent leg massage from brother Gregorio whilst Goyo chastised him for such defensive negligence.

Benitez hobbled out for the second round, still shaking out his right leg as if suffering from cramps or a similar muscular complaint. Moore missed with a jab and a right hand before throwing two left hooks downstairs, one of which appeared to land south of the border. Wilfred definitely thought so as he clutched his groin and continued to waggle the offending back leg whilst simultaneously appealing to the referee who chose to issue a standing count. When the action resumed, Moore unloaded again on an 'adversary' who seemed almost magnetically attracted to his own corner. Attempting to slip and dip, Benitez scarcely threw a punch in retaliation and when he was staggered by a chopping right hand,

Gerlando Lucia took his opportunity to step in and declare the desultory 'contest' at an end.

"I was surprised he stayed in the corner, like he did (with) Hamsho. I thought he'd change up his fight plan," Moore admitted to Chris Schenkel in the aftermath. "He's still a young man but he's a old fighter." With Wilfred unavailable for comment, Goyo offered his explanation for the nosediving trajectory of his youngest son's fistic prowess. "I think he got too many problems, you know..? He got too many problems in his house.. serious problems. I think his mind was over there. And the way he was talking today on television... he said, 'Every time I go to the ring, I think about my daughter and my wife.' That's not the way to talk (as) a fighter. When he go in the ring to think about his family - 'cos if he think about his family he can't win."

A couple of days later it was confirmed that Wilfred had broken his right ankle in 3 places as a result of the first-round knockdown. Before he even returned from Europe with his foot in a cast, the chairman of the Puerto Rican Boxing Commission declared that Benitez would be required to undergo an exhaustive medical examination due to his run of poor form. At only 25 years of age, after 51 professional fights, he appeared to be a spent force with little or no punch resistance. "But he's positive, he's in it to stay," claimed Wilfred's mother, Clara, after speaking with her son over the telephone whilst he received treatment in a Monte Carlo hospital. "He has no intention of retiring." Bizarrely, she quoted him as saying, "I lost but I feel as if I won."

Traditionally, fighters have always exhibited a mammoth capacity for self delusion and Wilfred's grip on reality was especially slender at the best of times. He would continue to fight because he knew nothing else but the world titles and the million-dollar paydays were gone forever. If he should have needed his predicament breaking down in the most stark and prosaic terms then the headline that appeared on the cover of 'Boxing News' the following week probably represented his best bet.

Quite simply, it read: 'BENITEZ HITS THE ROAD TO NOWHERE.'

16/ SLIGHT RETURN

Seeking to revive his ailing fortunes, Benitez signed a deal with Yamil Chade - a Lebanese born Puerto Rican based manager who had worked with the legendary Kid Gavilan and guided Wilfredo Gomez since his amateur days. By way of a confidence booster to kickstart the new alliance, Mauricio Bravo was dispatched in 2 rounds on the island of Aruba on March 30, 1985.[7] It constituted Wilfred's first stoppage win since the brutal KO of Maurice Hope 4 years earlier and the pattern continued when Danny Chapman was unable to answer the bell for the 8th round in Washington D.C on July 6. With 2 back to back knockouts on paper, Benitez was catapulted into a 10 rounder with the unbeaten Kevin Moley on a Madison Square Garden show headlined by Billy Costello and 'Lightning' Lonnie Smith on Wednesday, August 21. Moley - a good looking kid with a good looking record of 22-0 (19) - was the archetypal white American fighter in whom there was a degree of commercial value until he inevitably came unstuck against the first remotely world class opponent he faced. Or perhaps the first faded legend who had forgotten more about boxing than the untested Long Islander would ever know.

A new nadir beckoned when Benitez was floored in the opening 30 seconds by a short right hand although he jumped up as quickly as his knee had touched the canvas. At variance with rumours that he had looked bad in training and suffered several knockdowns in the gym, Wilfred came back strong, nailing Moley with a slew of

---

[7] When Benitez fought Kevin Moley on August 21 1986, commentator Al Bernstein made no mention of this fight and stated that Wilfred had only boxed once since losing to Moore.

concussive lead rights to arguably share the round. In the second, he came out dancing on solid legs that bore no resemblance to the shaky pins that had failed to hold him up in Monte Carlo. Midway through the session, a lead right/ left hand screw shot combo appeared to stun Moley who was bleeding freely from a cut over his right eye and missing copiously. If he had regarded the man in front of him as a toothless former name with which to fatten his resume then he had been disabused of the notion.

"Benitez seems to be growing with confidence as the fight wears on," remarked ESPN'S Charlie Steiner when the third round got underway. Undeniably, there was a verve about his work that had been absent since the Duran fight 3 and a half years ago when the world had been his oyster. More hittable than in days of yore, the former 3-time champ still possessed far too much craft for an ordinary fighter like Moley and by the 6th round he was giving the Teddy Atlas trained middleweight a boxing lesson. Visibly enjoying himself, Benitez skated the last 4 rounds with a virtuoso display of fleet footed guile and counterpunching accuracy although Moley never stopped trying. In seeking an explanation for the minor renaissance, it was worth noting the return of Emile Griffith who could be seen heaving his man aloft at the final bell. Scoring on the old fashioned 'rounds' system, Bernie Friiedkin and Simon Ramos each saw it for Benitez by margins of 7-3 whilst George DeGabriel had only given Moley 2 rounds. In terms of the bigger picture, it was almost certainly a false dawn but - for anyone outside of Kevin Moley's ample supporters club - it had been delightful to watch.

The dubious reward for a throwback performance came in the shape of streaking Canadian light middleweight puncher, Matthew Hilton, who had stopped Vito Antuofermo in his last fight. Wilfred and Matthew had much in common, both hailing as they did from dysfunctional fighting families in which a patriarchal obsession with ring glory would wreak a tumult of collateral damage. Arguably the best of 5 brothers, 4 of whom fought professionally, Hilton was undefeated in 19 contests and already a huge star in Montreal where the fight would be staged on February 15, 1986. At a press conference 4 days before the show, Don King informed the assembled scribes that he was expecting a live gate of 140 thousand U.S dollars with both fighters working on a percentage of the ticket sales. "We get next to nothing for the television rights but a sellout would assure both fighters handsome paydays," said the grandiloquent one. "This is a giant step for Matthew. Only Benitez stands between him and the world crown. There is much international excitement about this fight. I know everyone in Puerto Rico is excited. If Matthew wins, I'd like to present a big show for the world title here this summer in Montreal at the Olympic Stadium against Carlos Santos or Mike McCallum."

Firmly cast in the role of stepping stone, Benitez was first to enter the ring at the packed out Paul Sauvé Arena wearing a short white satin robe with shoulder pads. The juxtaposition of a red trim seemingly bore an intended resemblance to the Canadian flag - as if it might somehow placate the hostile crowd. In the notable absence of both Emile Griffith and his father, he was flanked by a pair of unknown Latino seconds.[8] When the 20-year-old

---

[8] During the ABC broadcast, Tim Ryan named Benitez' corner team as

hometown hero appeared to the strains of Richard Strauss, a deafening wall of noise erupted as he cut a swathe through the hordes. It was the kind of fanatical support that only Barry McGuigan - who would defend his WBA featherweight crown in Dublin several hours later - was capable of soliciting in the modern era. "With the fire inside a kid like Matthew Hilton, it certainly will help a great deal, Tim," said Gil Clancy when quizzed about the importance of the crowd by his CBS colleague. "And I don't think it can help Wilfred Benitez at all."

Maintaining his recent propensity for hitting the deck in the opening round, Wilfred was floored by a right hook to the body with only 100 seconds gone. Regaining his feet immediately, he slammed both gloves down on the top rope in frustration while Guy Jutras tolled the mandatory 8. Anticipating an early shower, Hilton attempted to hammer Benitez in the away corner with a smorgasbord of hooks and uppercuts but the latter's ingrained ring savvy prevented too many clean connections. "Benitez likes to stay on the ropes but as I said earlier, he'd better get off the ropes with this kid," warned Clancy. Just before the bell, an overhand right staggered the former champion who had yet to throw a meaningful punch. Taking the TV analyst's advice, Benitez used the ring to greater effect in Round 2 and had a better time of things until he was wobbled by a right uppercut / straight right followed by a left hook to the body. By all accounts, he had trained with due diligence but seemingly lacked the steam in his blows to keep Hilton at arm's length. In the third, Matthew nailed the veteran with a big left uppercut that rocked Benitez on his heels before following up with a pair of hooks to the body and a straight right hand that

Victor Montanez, Jim Pagan and Esteban Disaro.

jerked the older man's head back dramatically. "Tim, he has to have some chin to take those 2 shots..!" exclaimed Clancy.

Benitez boxed well in rounds 4 and 5 but struggled to impose himself and looked troubled whenever Hilton landed solidly. As he bobbed and weaved on the ropes, Tim Ryan made an interesting allusion to 'Wilfred's wife, Elizabeth, here as his manager, watching from ringside." It seemed reasonable to assume that her presence and Goyo's invisibility were not entirely unrelated. Hilton was docked a point at the end of the fifth for repeated low blows as Wilfred grimaced and touched his protective cup. But the tartan clad youngster could afford to lose points and was unquestionably breaking his man down. A left hook sent Benitez reeling midway through the 6th but Hilton was made to miss repeatedly as he flailed with both hands in an attempt to close the show. Showing great courage and resilience, the Puerto Rican fought his way out of a neutral corner, landing 'punches in bunches' on an opponent who had temporarily punched himself out. "Hilton is tired, he used up a lot..!" shouted Tim Ryan as the round came to a close.

"Benitez still looks rocky, Tim, legs aren't there," observed Gil Clancy at the beginning of the seventh which proved to be a quiet round as Hilton took a breather. He got his second wind in the eighth and immediately hurt Benitez with a series of left hooks and right hands that had the referee eyeing the situation closely. 'El Radar' shook his head defiantly but the up and comer was simply too strong for the erstwhile boy wonder whose best days had been swallowed by 2 decades of gruelling competition and a slew of questionable habits. The end came in the dying seconds of Round 9 when a huge left hook separated Benitez from his senses and sent him crashing to the canvas on his left side for the full count. The disturbing whiplash effect of the 'coup de grace' gave rise to concerns amongst all but the most insensitive observers but Wilfred was able to leave the ring under his own steam within minutes.

Anybody who truly cared about him could only hope it was for the last time.

17/ DON'T CRY FOR ME, ARGENTINA

After 55 professional fights in a 10-year career, Wilfred was showing increasing signs of behavioural disorder, according to his intimates. He suffered from memory loss and was prone to bouts of incoherent mania that would see him bouncing up and down and giggling uncontrollably. Some attributed his problems to an overuse of prescription medication while others blamed the more unsavoury fringes of the pharmaceutical industry. Be it an act of faith or merely a cynical desire to wring the last drops of revenue from an icon who needed saving from himself, Yamil Chade lined up a pair of 10 rounders against club fighter opposition in July and September. Benitez won both fights via the long route (vs Paul Whitaker and Harry Daniels) before events took a turn for the unexpected.

Allegedly, Chade sold his fighter's contract to an Argentinian promoter by name of Miguel Herrera for $40,000, although the genealogy of the transaction is unclear. There were unsubstantiated claims that Wilfred had gotten into some shady dealings and needed to leave Puerto Rico but the official explanation to his mother, who had begged him to quit after the Hilton fight, was simply that he wished 'to know the homeland of Carlos Monzon,' Argentina's greatest fighter. Herrera, for his part, intended to get his new acquisition a couple of wins before securing a world title fight and recouping his investment. Originally, Benitez was slated to face Miguel Angel Arroyo in Salta on November 14 but when Arroyo agreed to fight Lorenzo Garcia the day afterwards at Luna Park, in stepped Carlos Herrera, the former light middleweight contender who had lost a WBC title challenge to Maurice Hope back in 1980.

Making his way from Miami via San Salvador de Jujuy, Wilfred arrived in Salta on November 2 and was upbeat in his communications with the local press. "The fight with Herrera is much more important to me than you might think since I am working to get a new world title, so I cannot admit setbacks along the way." Unfortunately, there were setbacks regardless as the fight was postponed for a week amid rumours that the former star was in no fit state to compete and would return to Puerto Rico before the contract was honoured. 7 days later, the promoter was hit with an embargo regarding a dispute over a previous promotion, minutes before the doors of the Delmi Sports Centre were due to open. With all monies in the box office having been seized the show was postponed for another week as the promoter received medical treatment for a dramatic drop in blood pressure, presumably caused by anxiety. When the fighters finally faced off on November 28, Benitez was a woeful shadow of the wonderful boxer he had been in his pomp and received a one-sided thrashing from the opening gong. He was floored heavily in the third by what was simply described as 'a powerful blow to the jaw' and only saved by the bell according to the same report. With Herrera appealing to the referee to stop the fight, Wilfred endured another 9 minutes of unmitigated abuse before the ringside doctor effectively called a halt to proceedings at the end of the sixth round.[9] What happened afterwards has been subject to mythology and conjecture.

---

[9] Another online source states that the fight went into the 7th round. 'Moments into Round 7, Carlos backed Wilfred into the corner once again and threw a quick flurry that had Wilfred reeling and defenceless, where upon Referee Jose Maria Sosa stopped the bout'

It is generally claimed that Miguel Herrera didn't pay Benitez and stole his passport thus leaving him stranded in Salta where he lived on the streets for over a year, begging for sustenance as his mental state deteriorated. By this narrative, the locals got to know him well and would warmly refer to 'El Morenito' which loosely translates as 'the cute little brown guy.'[10] Endlessly walking up and down, he would tell anyone who stopped to listen that he was waiting for his purse and his passport was being held hostage. He crashed wherever he could, surviving on handouts and was frequently seen running through the streets at frantic speeds until he collapsed from exhaustion. Then when he came to, he would run some more.

Not so said Herrera. Although he admitted that the payment was delayed, Benitez eventually received every cent of his contracted $14,000 purse claimed the promoter. The fighter had stayed in Argentina voluntarily because he was convinced he would be arrested for an outstanding debt as soon as he set foot on Puerto Rican soil. Furthermore, said Herrera, he had picked up Wilfred's hotel bills for months on end and his mother had cooked the visitor's meals. His mistake, he conceded, had been to give Benitez money in order to avoid dealing with him. Whenever Wilfred showed up at the promoter's office, the latter would instruct his staff to give him a few pesos but not to let him in. "The mistake was mine. I gave him money so I didn't have to see him. At one point, my family told me, 'Benitez or us. It's driving you crazy..!'" As if to lend authenticity to his version of events, Herrera offered a bizarre anecdote. His father had died during the extended saga and when they held the wake in the family

---

[10] Source – 'Malfunctioning Radar' – Jose Corpas April 2017

living room, Wilfred stood and stared at the open casket for 24 hours without flinching, as if locked in ring centre in the lustre of his prime.

Yet another source suggested that Herrera had withheld a substantial portion of the purse and retained Benitez' passport due to his chagrin at being 'sold a bill of goods' in light of his non-performance. A local journalist said the ex- champ needed helping into the ring on the night and had actually failed the pre-fight medical. An equilibrium test required the fighters to form an X across their chests whilst standing on one leg and Wilfred couldn't do it, he alleged. Everyone in the room is reported to have looked at each for a moment as if waiting for somebody to speak up and do the right thing but nobody did. Whatever the truth, holding Benitez prisoner seemed to offer little advantage to Herrera since the Salta Boxing Commission had revoked his license immediately after the fight. And so there were those who insisted that tales of the 28-year old's dereliction during this period were exaggerated and that he lived in a nice apartment for much of the time, earning money as a boxing instructor at 'Club Athletico Aqua Calientes.' Adding to the confusion was his wife Elizabeth's contention that her husband had been promised 25 thousand dollars as per the original contract. According to at least one writer, she had instructed Wilfred not to come home until he had collected the 25 grand in its entirety.

Having not heard from their most famous son for several months, the Benitez family put pressure on the Puerto Rican government to send an envoy to ensure his safe return. Accordingly, in either December 1987 or March 1988 depending on the account, a Mr. Leonard Gonzalez arrived in Salta to collect the depleted national treasure.

Benitez is said to have been 'underweight, malnourished and incoherent' when Gonzalez found him. Seeking to underline his position as a caring benefactor, Miguel Herrera later claimed that the man sent by the Puerto Rican authorities proffered a cheque and asked, "What do we owe you for your troubles, Mr. Herrera...?"

Upon his return, Wilfred spent 2 weeks in hospital and his boxing license was permanently cancelled by the local commission. It is said he was offered a job as a trainer to 'Olympic hopefuls' for $800 a month but there is no evidence of such an arrangement coming to fruition. No doubt the offer was well intentioned but, even with a clean bill of cerebral health, it seems unlikely that 'El Radar' would have flourished in the role since great fighters tend not to have patience with the mere mortals who lack their genius. Unconscionably, he returned to the ring in 1990 and recorded a 7th round stoppage over a 'tomato can' named Ariel Conde in a Phoenix motel. Conde, alternatively known as Henry Perez, had been flattened in all but one of previous 11 fights and would retire in 1997 with 30 losses and a draw. 2 months later, Benitez lost a split decision to 'Irish' Pat Lawlor in Tucson, despite the presence of the great Manny Steward in his corner. In Lawlor's next fight, Roberto Duran bailed out in the sixth round with an injured shoulder thus cementing perhaps the two most disingenuously flattering wins in boxing history.

Our hero got his hand raised one more time when he beat Sam Wilson in Denver before journeying to Canada to make his final bow against an unremarkable scrapper from Minnesota who answered to the name of Scott Papasodora. According to a report in the Winnipeg Free Press, Benitez was 'slow, almost plodding. He was often off balance and his punches had no sting. By the end of the fight, he bloodied Papasodora's nose and appeared as if he could go all night. But after losing all the early rounds his conditioning hardly mattered.' Bloody nose or not, Papasodora got the decision and effectively drove a final nail into the coffin one of the more illustrious careers in the annals of Hispanic boxing. By way of a yardstick for how far the mighty had fallen, Scott had been inactive for 2 years and would lose his next 3 bouts before retiring in December 1991. Seemingly a lifetime ago, it had taken men of the calibre of Sugar Ray Leonard and Thomas Hearns to put digits on the right hand side of the Benitez curriculum vitae. 6 days after his 32nd birthday, it was painfully apparent that any semi competent prospect with a pulse would be favoured to do the same.

Upon his return from Manitoba, Wilfred moved back into his parents' house, having filed for divorce immediately after the Lawlor fight. Of an estimated 6-8 million dollars in ring earnings there was apparently nothing left and quite what happened to the various properties, assets and trust funds in the fighter's name remains a mystery. Historically, Goyo has taken the lion share of the blame for the wanton exploitation of his fourth born son whilst the family insist that his ex - wife was a gold digger. Perhaps Wilfred, as a grown man, should be obliged to accept a degree of responsibility for his own affairs but any such logic is compromised by the suspicion that he was differently abled in some way or other. In the 21st century, it seems unlikely he would have escaped a diagnosis of mild autism or ADHD and his academic education had been threadbare at best. The trauma that his still developing brain was subjected to throughout the innumerable back garden gym wars can hardly have prepared him for anything besides fistic immortality and a premature disintegration of mind, body and soul.

Admittedly, there is another school of thought which states that some fighters are simply more susceptible to long term neurological damage on account of their genetics. Citing the sprightliness of the late Jake LaMotta in his 90s, proponents of this theory conclude that nobody could have saved Wilfred Benitez from the ravages of a sport that frequently stretches the very definition of the word. Conceivably, they speak the truth but having forged an affection for my subject in the course of this writing, it remains hard to shake the conviction that somebody at least ought to have tried.

18/ IN HIS OWN TIME

On March 5, 1996, Gregorio Benitez Sr died suddenly of a brain haemorrhage, the day before the 20-year anniversary of his son's greatest triumph. 2 years earlier he had split with Clara with whom he is said to have argued frequently over the handling of Wilfred's career. By now, the latter had been diagnosed with chronic traumatic encephalopathy, a degenerative brain condition that is commonly if not exclusively associated with former fighters in their dotage. Weighing 70 pounds over his best fighting weight, he was almost entirely dependent on the $1,125 a month he received from the Puerto Rican government. Senator Ramon Luis Rivera, who had sponsored a bill to give the ex- champion an annual pension of $7,200 was keen to waylay any accusations that his penury had been self inflicted. "Wilfred lost everything. Even if he lost the money, he brought fame to Puerto Rico at one time and many people enjoyed that fame. Now he's in a critical situation, why not give him a little help..?"

In June, Wilfred was inducted into the International Boxing Hall of Fame, the ultimate accolade in an industry that had begun to hand out world titles like supermarket loyalty cards. Pictured at the closing ceremony on a sunny afternoon with Marvin Hagler, he resembles a perfectly healthy, if portly, ex - champ. 5 months later, Clara went to the kitchen to cut her son a slice of cake and returned to find him collapsed on the living room floor, vomiting and convulsing before he passed out. With everybody fearing the worst, he was taken to the University Hospital in Rio Piedras where he remained in a coma for several days. Although he never fully recovered, he was well enough to attend the HOF celebrations the following year for the induction of his one-time rival, Sugar Ray Leonard. At this point, according to the New York Times, 'he could talk without slurring his words and walk two steps without faltering.' Although his ex - wife still lived right across the street, visits from his 12-year-old daughter had become increasingly sporadic said Clara when expounding on Wilfred's state of mind to a journalist. "Sometimes, he is so negative. He says his sight isn't good. He says God is punishing him. I tell him God will help him but in His own time." Suggesting that he wasn't the only one suffering from memory loss, Wilfred chipped in, "I've been talking care of myself. I'm retired. Nobody is thinking about me like before."

Also living at home with Mom were Gregorio Jr and Frankie, who both suffered from less severe but still appreciable forms of dementia puglistica. Shortly after Frankie's 40th birthday, Wilfred began to break things - perhaps lashing out at a God who had forsaken him - and Clara was advised to put him in care for the safety of all involved. At Hogar San Augustin y Teresa, he tended to enjoy his celebrity amongst 14 other residents, all male with varying types of mental disorders. Sometimes a fellow patient or a member of staff would ask him to shadow-box and, on a good day, he would oblige to rapturous applause. When he sat down after these impromptu displays and whispered, "I would like to start boxing again," it was hard to tell if he was serious or not.

And so, for the next 10 years, he ricocheted between the care of medical professionals in assisted living and his mother and sister during spells at home. When Sugar Ray Leonard paid a visit to San Augustin in 2002, Wilfred did not immediately recognise the man who had dealt him his first professional loss. Describing the facility as a place with 'the odour of sickness and death in every corridor', Leonard recounted the bittersweet reunion in his autobiography. 'We reached a room that was almost dark, its lone inhabitant sitting in a rocking chair, his face and stomach bloated, his eyes staring blankly into space..... I was devastated. It was one thing to meet fighters from earlier eras and see the harm our sport can inflict. It was quite another to witness the effects on someone from my era.' When it became apparent that the television room had been set up for a nostalgic screening of their 1979 title fight, Sugar Ray was apprehensive but saw 'a spark in his eyes' as Wilfred sat mesmerised by the moving images of his younger self on screen. When it was over, he whispered softly, "Su...gar... I want you to know that I no train for that fight." He had lost so much since that fateful night in Las Vegas but his pride was evidently still hanging in there.

When Clara passed away on July 25, 2008, Wilfred's sister, Yvonne, became his sole carer in the single storey brick house in St. Just. His health continued to deteriorate after being diagnosed with diabetes and suffering a stroke but on lucid days he was still capable of surprising people 'by singing Hector Lavoe songs and cheering for Miguel Cotto' according to Jose Corpas in an article published online in 2017. On the worst days, he was cocooned in a dark incommunicable despair that brought an overwhelming desire for oblivion. "He told me to kill him with a gun," Yvonne was quoted as saying.

In 2018, after the family home was irreparably damaged by Hurricane Maria, Yvonne relocated her sick brother to Chicago with the help of former pro light middleweight, Luis Mateo. Mateo, an old spar mate of Wilfred's who boxed in good company in the 70s and 80s, had been reunited with his friend during his involvement in a recovery effort for victims of the hurricane. Seeing his contemporary bedridden and frail, having lost the motor skills required to move his fingers, Luis pledged to bring him to the States where he would receive better medical attention. "I feel like I'm the one who hurt him," admitted Mateo. "I beat the shit out of him in training, and I see him like this, and I think 'Oh God, why did I do this..?'"

Yvonne was sceptical but Mateo was as good as his word, raising funds amongst Chicago's Puerto Rican community in order to bring Wilfred to the 'Windy City' on June 1, 2018. He spent the first week in hospital before sister and brother moved into a West Side apartment. "He looks better than when we came," remarked Yvonne in an interview with the Chicago Tribune. "I noticed that he's gaining weight, he's more alert and he wants to talk." Also instrumental in the bid to salvage what remained of a national treasure was one time WBA Heavyweight title challenger, Fres Oquendo, who set up a programme to provide water, food and clothing to the people in his ravaged homeland. With his own career on ice due to legal wrangling, Wilfred became the focus of his charitable efforts. "My Dad would tell me about him when I was growing up," he told Sky Sports in August. "I was shocked that I had the opportunity to help him. Nobody was able to help this great champion of Puerto Rico. I was able to assist him and his family by bringing him to Chicago, the city I love and where I was raised. This makes me feel like I've done something great in my life."

The hankering to have done something great with one's life was presumably the driving force behind a father's decision to turn three teenaged sons professional whilst still in the throes of puberty. As unkind as posterity has been to Gregorio 'Goyo' Benitez, it is only fair to point out that the circumstances which lead to the worst case scenario that Wilfred now inhabits were hardly unique. He was not the first 15-year-old to be thrust into the hurt business at the behest of a draconian father and exposed to an overabundance of hard sparring. And neither is he the first fighter to wind up in such a terrible state of paraplegic purgatory. Those who are learned on the scientific aspects have campaigned for professional boxing to be outlawed for decades without significant momentum or success. Still others suggest the introduction of new rules and protocols that would render the fight game about as commercially viable as a prostitute who specialises in hugs. The reality of two supremely drilled athletes hitting one another with 8 or 10oz gloves for up to 36 minutes will always carry inherent risks of death, serious injury and irreversible brain damage. 'Fighters know the risks' say the insiders, although the likelihood of the average boxer being well versed in the intricacies of neurology seems rather remote. Crucially, fighters believe that it won't happen to them. And so when confronted with the disquieting example of a Wilfred Benitez, they point to his storied indifference to serious training as if seeking to prove that a lack of application was solely to blame for his present day condition. Rumours of the triple crown champ's predilection for loose women and powdered stimulants are ultimately lacking in corroboration and any attempt to turn the Wilfred Benitez story into an anti - drugs narrative would be disingenuous at best.

The late Gene Tunney espoused that a successful prize-fighter should have two aims in mind: to make money and to avoid harm. By such a maxim alone, the career of

Wilfred Benitez might be considered an abject failure but something deep in the blood and marrow of the true boxing fan curdles at the suggestion. Being of a more sentimental bent, we prefer to remember a defensive genius and sublime counterpuncher who was so ludicrously adept at the rudiments of boxing that it often bored him. In addition to the astonishing gifts that made him the best young fighter in the sport's rich history, I will also remember his childlike innocence and the graciousness he displayed in victory and defeat. While he lays immobile, half blind and mute on the verge of his 64th birthday, those who love Wilfred Benitez have not given up hope that he will walk again someday with sufficient therapy and treatment. The odds are longer than any he ever faced in the ring but, regardless of the outcome, his most unbreakable legacy will stand forever.

ACKNOWLEDGEMENTS:

Jose Corpas for a fine article that helped me get started.

Mick Guilfoyle as ever for being my mirror.

The New York Times

Sports Illustrated.

The Washington Post.

Senor Pepe for a wealth of knowledge on matters Benitez.

Natalie Bleau – without whom none of this would have gotten past first base.

Printed in Great Britain
by Amazon

26795758R00090